ROUGH GUIDES **PHRASEBOOK**

PORTUGUESE

ROUGH GUIDES

Contacting the Editors

Every effort has been made to provide accurate information in this publication, but changes are inevitable. The publisher cannot be responsible for any resulting loss, inconvenience or injury.
We would appreciate it if readers would call our attention to any errors or outdated information. We also welcome your suggestions; if you come across a relevant expression not in our phrase book, please contact us at: **mail@uk.roughguides.com**

Cover & Interior Design: Slawomir Krajewski
Head of Production: Rebeka Davies
Production Manager: Rebecca Hancock
Picture Researcher: Slawomir Krajewski
Cover Photo: all shutterstock

Interior Photos: all shutterstock

CONTENTS

INTRODUCTION

Pronunciation 7
How to use the App 12
Grammar 14

PRACTICALITIES

THE BASICS **20**
NUMBERS **20**
NEED TO KNOW 20
Ordinal Numbers 22
TIME **23**
NEED TO KNOW 23
DAYS **24**
NEED TO KNOW 24
Dates 25
Months 25
Seasons 26
Holidays 27
ARRIVAL & DEPARTURE **28**

NEED TO KNOW 28
Border Control 28
MONEY **30**
NEED TO KNOW 30
At the Bank 31
CONVERSATION **33**
NEED TO KNOW 34
Language Difficulties 36
Making Friends 37
Travel Talk 38
Personal 39
Work & School 40
Weather 41

ON THE WAY

GETTING AROUND **44**
NEED TO KNOW 44
Tickets 46
Airport Transfer 48
Checking In 50
Luggage 52
Finding your Way 53
Train 54
Departures 55
On Board 56
Bus 56
Metro 58
Boat & Ferry 59

Taxi 60
Bicycle & Motorbike 62
Car Hire 63
Fuel Station 65
Asking Directions 66
Parking 66
Breakdown & Repair 68
Accidents 70
PLACES TO STAY **71**
NEED TO KNOW 71
Somewhere to Stay 72
At the Hotel 73
Price 75

Preferences	76	Phone	91
Questions	77	Telephone Etiquette	93
Problems	78	Fax	94
Checking Out	80	Post	95
Renting	81	**SIGHTSEEING**	**97**
Domestic Items	83	NEED TO KNOW	97
At the Hostel	84	Tourist Information	97
Going Camping	86	On Tour	98
COMMUNICATIONS	**87**	Seeing the Sights	99
NEED TO KNOW	87	Religious Sites	101
Online	89		
Social Media	90		

LEISURE TIME

SHOPPING	**104**	Newsstand & Tobacconist	122
NEED TO KNOW	104	Photography	123
At the Shops	105	Souvenirs	124
Ask an Assistant	107	**SPORT & LEISURE**	**126**
Personal Preferences	109	NEED TO KNOW	126
Paying & Bargaining	109	Watching Sport	127
Making a Complaint	111	Playing Sport	128
Services	112	At the Beach/Pool	130
Hair & Beauty	113	Winter Sports	132
Antiques	115	Out in the Country	133
Clothing	116	**TRAVELING**	
Colors	117	**WITH CHILDREN**	**136**
Clothes & Accessories	118	NEED TO KNOW	136
Fabric	120	Out & About	137
Shoes	120	Baby Essentials	138
Sizes	121	Babysitting	139

SAFE TRAVEL

EMERGENCIES	**142**	**HEALTH**	**147**
NEED TO KNOW	142	NEED TO KNOW	147
POLICE	**144**	Finding a Doctor	147
NEED TO KNOW	144	Symptoms	149
Crime & Lost Property	145	Conditions	150

Treatment 151
Hospital 152
Dentist 152
Gynecologist 152
Optician 153
Payment & Insurance 153
PHARMACY **154**
NEED TO KNOW 154

What to Take 155
Basic Supplies 157
Child Health &
Emergency 159
DISABLED TRAVELERS **160**
NEED TO KNOW 160
Asking for Assistance 160

FOOD

EATING OUT **164**
NEED TO KNOW 164
Where to Eat 166
Reservations &
Preferences 167
How to Order 168
Cooking Methods 171
Dietary Requirements 172
Dining with Children 173
How to Complain 174
Paying 175
MEALS & COOKING **176**
Breakfast 176
Appetizers 179
Soup 179
Fish & Seafood 181

Meat & Poultry 183
Vegetables & Staples 185
Fruit 187
Cheese 188
Dessert 189
Sauces & Condiments 190
At the Market 190
In the Kitchen 192
DRINKS **194**
NEED TO KNOW 194
Non-alcoholic Drinks 196
Apéritifs, Cocktails &
Liqueurs 197
Beer 198
Wine 199
ON THE MENU **201**

PEOPLE

GOING OUT **230**
NEED TO KNOW 230
Entertainment 230
Nightlife 232
ROMANCE **234**

NEED TO KNOW 234
The Dating Game 234
Accepting & Rejecting 236
Getting Intimate 237
Sexual Preferences 237

DICTIONARY

ENGLISH–PORTUGUESE **240**

PORTUGUESE–ENGLISH **265**

PRONUNCIATION

This section is designed to make you familiar with the sounds of Portuguese using our simplified phonetic transcription. You'll find the pronunciation of the Portuguese letters and sounds explained below, together with their 'imitated' equivalents. This system is used throughout the phrase book; simply read the pronunciation as if it were English, noting any special rules below.

Stressed syllables are indicated by underlining in the phonetics. Portuguese has four accent marks; **acute (´)**, **grave (`)**, **circumflex (^)**, and **tilde (˜)**. Accent marks are used to indicate a stressed syllable, or to distinguish between words with the same spelling but with a different pronunciation and meaning: for example, **é** pronounced 'eh' (meaning **is**) and **e** pronounced 'ee' (meaning **and**).

There are some differences in vocabulary and pronunciation between the Portuguese spoken in Portugal and that spoken in Brazil, although people in either country can easily understand the other. This book is specifically geared to travelers in Portugal.

CONSONANTS

Letter	Approximate Pronunciation	Symbol	Example	Pronunciation
b	1. as in English	b	bota	_bah_ • tuh
	2. between vowels, as in English but softer	b	bebida	beh • _bee_ • duh
c	1. before e or i, like s in same	s	centro	_sehn_ • troh
	2. like k in kit	k	como	_koh_ • moh
ç	like s in same	s	cabeça	kuh • _beh_ • suh
ch	like sh in shower	sh	chave	shahv
d	1. as in English	d	diário	dee • _ah_ • ree • oo
	2. like th in theater	th	medo	_meh_ • thoo

Letter	Approximate Pronunciation	Symbol	Example	Pronunciation
g	1. before e or i, like s in pleasure	zs	gelo	_zseh_ • loo
	2. before a, o or u as in English	g	guerra	geh • rruh
h	always silent		história	ee • _staw_ • ree • uh
j	like s in pleasure	zs	juiz	zsoo • _eezs_
l	1. as in English	l	luz	looz
	2. before h (lh), like ll in millions	ly	milho	_mee_ • lyoo
m	1. as in English	m	camera	_cuh_ • meh • ruh
	2. at the end of a word, m is nasalized: see p11			
n	1. as in English	n	caneta	kuh • _neh_ • tah
	2. before h (nh), like ny in canyon	ny	banho	_buh_ • nyoo
qu	1. before e and i, like k in kite	k	quente	kint
	2. before a and o like qu in queen	kw	qualidade	kwah • lee • dahd
r	1. strongly trilled	rr	rio	_rree_ • oo
	2. lightly trilled	r	para	puh • _ruh_
s	1. like s in same	s	sua	_soo_ • uh
	2. between vowels, like z in zebra	z	camisa	kuh • mee • zuh
x	1. like sh in sheep	sh	peixe	paysh
	2. like s in same	s	próximo	_praw_ • see • moo
	3. like z in lazy	z	exame	ee • _zuhm_

Letters **f**, **m**, **p**, **t** and **z** are pronounced as in English. Letters **k**, **w** and **y** are used only in foreign loan words.

VOWELS

Letter	Approximate Pronunciation	Symbol	Example	Pronunciation
a, ã, â	like a in about	uh	**anos**	_uh_ • nooz
á, à	like a in father	ah	**farmácia**	fuhrmah • see • _uh_
e	1. like e in get	eh	**esta**	_eh_ • stuh
	2. like ee in eel	ee	**exame**	ee • _zuhm_
	3. silent at the end of a word		**leite**	_layt_
	4. occasionally, like i in inn	i	**antes**	_ahn_ • tis
	5. when combined with the letter l, like ay in say	ay	**leite**	_layt_
é	like e in get	eh	**esta**	_eh_ • stuh
ê	like i in inn	i	**mês**	miz
i, í	like ee in eel	ee	**sim**	seeng
o	1. like au in caught	au	**onda**	_aun_ • duh
	2. at the end of a word, like oo in boo	oo	**gato**	_gah_ • too
oi	like oy in coy	oy	**doi**	doy
ó	like aw in paw	aw	**história**	ee • _staw_ • ree • uh
ô	like u in put	oah	**avô**	uh • _voah_
u	1. like oo in boo	oo	**uva**	_oo_ • vuh
	2. silent after g and q		**guerra**	_geh_ • rruh
ú	like oo in boo	oo	**úmido**	_oo_ • mee • thoo

When a vowel has an accent, you must stress the syllable in the word that contains the accented vowel.

NASAL SOUNDS

Some nasal sounds are produced when a vowel is followed by the letter **m**. This nasal sound is also found when a combination of certain vowels are used (**ãe**, **ão**, **õe**). These nasal sounds produce either an **ng** sound (e.g., tying) or an **oam** sound (e.g., foam) with the speaker barely pronouncing the **g** or **m**.

Letter	Approximate Pronunciation	Symbol	Example	Pronunciation
ãe	like ayin in saying	**eng**	**mãe**	*meng*
** aõ**	like oam in foam	**ohm**	**cão**	*kohm*
õe	like oing in boing	**oing**	**milhões**	*mee • <u>lyoings</u>*
am	at the end of a word, like oam in foam otherwise not nasal: see p8	**ohm**	**falam**	<u>*fah*</u> *• loam*
om	like ong in gong	**ohng**	**som**	*sohng*
em	like aying in saying	**eng**	**bem**	*beng*
im	like ing in typing	**ing**	**assim**	*uh • <u>sing</u>*
oi, oy	like w followed by the a in hat	**wah**	**moi**	*mwah*
ou, oû	like o in move or oo in hoot	**oo**	**nouveau**	*noo • voh*
ui	approximately wee in between	**wee**	**traduire**	*trah • dweer*

There are over 230 million speakers of Portuguese worldwide. Portuguese is the sixth most spoken language in the world, and there are 188 million speakers of Portuguese in South America alone. It is the official language of Angola, Brazil, Cape Verde, East Timor, Guinea-Bissau, Mozambique, Portugal and São Tomé and Príncipe. Portuguese is also spoken in Macao, though Cantonese is the language of commerce. There are about 400,000 Portuguese speakers in the United States.

HOW TO USE THE APP

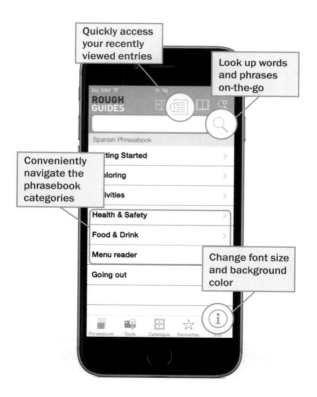

Quickly access your recently viewed entries

Look up words and phrases on-the-go

Conveniently navigate the phrasebook categories

Change font size and background color

Save the most useful everyday words and phrases to your Favorites

Use the Flash Cards Quiz to learn and memorize new words easily

Take all digital advantages of the app: listen to words and phrases pronounced by native speakers

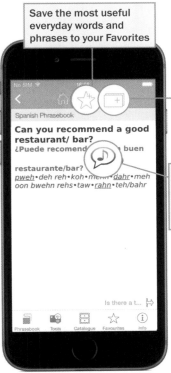

To learn how to Activate the app, see the inside back cover of this phrasebook.

GRAMMAR

In Portuguese, there are three ways to say 'you' (taking different verb forms):

In Portugal, **tu** is used when talking to a relative your age or younger, a close friend, a child and between young people; in Brazil, **tu** is hardly ever used. **Tu** refers to just one person at a time, and it takes the second person singular form of the verb.

In Portugal, **você(s)** is used in more formal situations, between people who don't know each other well and as a sign of respect for family members, anyone older than you, more educated than you or in business. In most parts of Brazil, **você** is predominantly used when talking to anyone, regardless of age or class, even in cases when **tu** would be used in Portugal. **Você(s)** takes either the third person singular or the third person plural of the verb depending on whether you're referring to one person (**você**) or more than one person (**vocês**).

The most formal way of saying 'you' is **o(s) senhor(es)** to a man (men) and **a(s) senhora(s)** to a woman (women). This is the case in both Portugal and Brazil. **O(s) senhor(es)** and **a(s) senhora(s)** take either the third person singular of the verb or the third person plural depending on whether you're referring to one person (**o senhor/a senhora**) or more than one person (**os senhores/as senhoras**).

REGULAR VERBS

Here are three of the main categories of regular verbs in the present tense:

	-ar falar	-er comer	-ir cobrir
eu	falo	como	cubro
tu	falas	comes	cobres
ele/ela/você	fala	come	cobre
nós	falamos	comemos	cobrimos

| vós | falais | comeis | cobris |
| eles/elas/vocês | falam | comem | cobrem |

IRREGULAR VERBS

In Portuguese there are two main verbs meaning 'to be', both of which are irregular:

Ser indicates a permanent state:
Sou inglês. I'm English.
É portuguesa. She is Portuguese.

Estar indicates movement or a temporary state:
Está doente. He is sick [ill].
Estou a passear. I am walking.

NOUNS & ARTICLES

Nouns in Portuguese are either masculine or feminine.
Masculine nouns usually end in **-o** and feminine nouns in **-a**.
Normally nouns that end in a vowel become plural by adding an **-s**.
Articles must agree with the noun to which they refer in gender and number.
Indefinite: **um carro** (a car); **uns carros** (some cars); **uma casa** (a house); **umas casas** (some houses)
Definite: **o carro** (the cars); **os carros** (some cars); **a casa** (the house); **as casas** (the houses)

WORD ORDER

In Portuguese, the conjugated verb comes after the subject.
Maria fala inglês. Maria speaks English.

To ask a question, reverse the order of the subject and verb, change your intonation or use key question words such as **quando** (when).
Quando abre o museu? When does the museum open?
Literally translates to: 'When opens the museum?'
É portuguesa? Is she Portuguese?
Literally: She is Portuguese? This is a statement that becomes a question by raising the pitch of the last syllable of the sentence.

NEGATION

To form a negative sentence, add **não** (not) before the verb.

Fumamos.	We smoke.
Não fumamos.	We don't smoke.

IMPERATIVES

Imperative sentences, commands, are formed by adding the appropriate ending to the stem of the verb.

Fale!	Speak!
Abra a janela, por favor.	Open the window, please.

COMPARATIVE & SUPERLATIVE

The comparative is usually formed by adding **mais** (more) or **menos** (less) before the adjective or noun. The superlative is formed by adding the appropriate definite article (**o/os, a/as**) and **mais** (the most) or **menos** (the least).

alto	mais alto	o mais alto
tall	taller	tallest
caro	menos caro	o menos caro
expensive	less expensive	least expensive

POSSESSIVE PRONOUNS

Pronouns serve as substitutes for specific nouns and must agree with the noun in gender and number.

meu *m*/minha *f*	mine
teu *m*/tua *f*	yours
seu *m*/sua *f*	yours (formal)
nosso *m*/nossa *f*	ours
vosso *m*/vossa *f*	yours (plural)

Example: **Esse assento é meu.** That seat is mine.

ADJECTIVES

Adjectives describe nouns and must agree with the noun in gender and number. In Portuguese, adjectives usually come after the noun. Masculine adjectives usually end in **-o**, feminine adjectives in **-a**. If the masculine form ends in **-e (intellegente)** or with a consonant (**fácil**), the feminine form is generally the same.

O filho/A filha é amável.	Your son/daughter is nice.
O mar/A flor azul.	The blue ocean/flower.

ADVERBS & ADVERBIAL EXPRESSIONS

Adverbs are used to describe verbs. Some adverbs are formed by adding **-mente** to the singular feminine form of the adjective. Example: **sincera + mente = sinceramente**
The following are some common adverbial time expressions:

agora	now
ainda não	not yet
ainda	still
nunca	never
sempre	always

PRACTICALITIES

THE BASICS	20
ARRIVAL & DEPARTURE	28
MONEY	30
CONVERSATION	33

THE BASICS

NUMBERS

NEED TO KNOW

0	**zero** *zeh • roo*
1	**um** *m*/**uma** *f* *oong/oo • muh*
2	**dois** *m*/**duas** *f* *doyz/thoo • uhz*
3	**três** *trehz*
4	**quatro** *kwah • troo*
5	**cinco** *seeng • koo*
6	**seis** *sayz*
7	**sete** *seht*
8	**oito** *oy • too*
9	**nove** *nawv*
10	**dez** *dehz*
11	**onze** *aunz*
12	**doze** *dauz*

13	**treze**
	trehz
14	**catorze**
	kuh • taurz
15	**quinze**
	keengz
16	**dezasseis**
	dehz • eh • sayz
17	**dezassete**
	dehz • eh • seht
18	**dezoito**
	dehz • oy • too
19	**dezanove**
	deh • zuh • nawv
20	**vinte**
	veent
21	**vinte e um** *m*/**uma** *f*
	veent ee oong/oo • muh
22	**vinte e dois** *m*/**duas** *f*
	veent ee doyz/thoo • uhz
30	**trinta**
	treeng • tuh
31	**trinta e um** *m*/**uma** *f*
	treeng • tuh ee oong/oo • muh
40	**quarenta**
	kwuh • rehn • tuh
50	**cinquenta**
	seeng • kwehn • tuh
60	**sessenta**
	seh • sehn • tuh
70	**setenta**
	seh • tehn • tuh

80	**oitenta**
	oy • tehn • tuh
90	**noventa**
	noo • vehn • tuh
100	**cem**
	sehn
101	**cento e um** *m*/**uma** *f*
	sehn • too ee oong/oo • muh
200	**duzentos** *m*/**duzentas** *f*
	doo • zehn • tooz/doo • zehn • tuhz
500	**quinhentos** *m*/**quinhentas** *f*
	kee • nyehn • tooz/kee • nyehn • tuhz
1,000	**mil**
	meel
10,000	**dez mil**
	dehz meel
1,000,000	**um milhão**
	oong mee • lyohm

ORDINAL NUMBERS

first	**o primeiro** *m*/**a primeira** *f*
	oo pree • may • roo/uh pree • may • ruh
second	**o segundo** *m*/**a segunda** *f*
	oo seh • goon • doo/uh seh • goon • duh
third	**o terceiro** *m*/**a terceira** *f*
	f oo tehr • say • roo/uh tehr • say • ruh
fourth	**o quarto** *m*/**a quarta** *f*
	oo kwahr • too/uh kwahr • tuh
fifth	**o quinto** *m* /**a quinta** *f*
	oo keen • too/uh keen • tuh

once	**uma vez**
	_oo_ • muh vehz
twice	**duas vezes**
	thoo • uhz _veh_ • zehz
three times	**três vezes**
	trehz _veh_ • zehz

TIME

NEED TO KNOW

What time is it?	**As horas, por favor?**
	uhz _aw_ • ruhz poor fuh • _vaur_
It's noon [mid-day].	**É meio-dia.**
	eh _may_ • oo _dee_ • uh
At midnight.	**À meia-noite.**
	ah _may_ • uh noyt
From nine o'clock to five o'clock.	**Das nove às cinco horas.**
	duhz nawv ahz _seeng_ • koo _aw_ • ruhz
Twenty [after] past four.	**Quatro e vinte.**
	kwah • troo ee veent
A quarter to nine.	**Um quarto para as nove.**
	oong _kwahr_ • too _puh_ • ruh uhz nawv
5:30 a.m./p.m.	**Cinco e meia de manhã/da tarde.**
	seeng • koo ee _may_ • uh deh muh • _nyuh/_ duh tahrd

In Portugal, digital time is on the 24-hour clock, but time is not referred to in that way. The Portuguese would not say it's '13:00,' in speech but rather they would express the hour along with the time of day, i.e. 'one in the afternoon' (**uma hora da tarde**).

DAYS

NEED TO KNOW

Monday	**segunda-feira**
	seh • <u>goon</u> • duh <u>fay</u> • ruh
Tuesday	**terça-feira**
	<u>tehr</u> • suh <u>fay</u> • ruh
Wednesday	**quarta-feira**
	<u>kwahr</u> • tuh <u>fay</u> • ruh
Thursday	**quinta-feira**
	<u>keen</u> • tuh <u>fay</u> • ruh
Friday	**sexta-feira**
	<u>say</u> • stuh <u>fay</u> • ruh
Saturday	**sábado**
	<u>sah</u> • buh • thoo
Sunday	**domingo**
	doo • <u>meeng</u> • goo

Portuguese calendars go from Monday to Sunday. When giving dates, the Portuguese give the day first, then the month, then the year (e.g. 1 May 2009 or 1/5/2009).

DATES

yesterday	**ontem**
	awn • teng
today	**hoje**
	auzseh
tomorrow	**amanhã**
	uh • muh • _nuh_
day	**o dia**
	oo _dee_ • uh
week	**a semana**
	uh seh • _muh_ • nuh
month	**o mês**
	oo mehz
year	**o ano**
	oo _uh_ • noo

MONTHS

January	**Janeiro**
	zher • _nay_ • roo
February	**Fevereiro**
	feh • _vray_ • roo

March	**Março**
	mahr • soo
April	**Abril**
	uh • breel
May	**Maio**
	meye • oo
June	**Junho**
	zsoo • nyoo
July	**Julho**
	zsoo • lyoo
August	**Agosto**
	uh • gaus • too
September	**Setembro**
	seh • tehm • broo
October	**Outubro**
	aw • too • broo
November	**Novembro**
	noo • vehm • broo
December	**Dezembro**
	deh • zehm • broo

SEASONS

the spring	**a primavera**
	uh pree • muh • veh • ruh
the summer	**o verão**
	oo vrohm
the fall [autumn]	**o outono**
	oo aw • too • noo
the winter	**o inverno**
	oo eeng • verr • noo

The dates of **Carnaval** are based on the dates of Lent and Easter, and therefore change every year. **Carnaval** starts on the Saturday before Ash Wednesday and lasts until Ash Wednesday.

HOLIDAYS

January 1	New Year's Day
January 6	Epiphany
April 25	Freedom Day
May 1	May Day
June 10	Camões Day
August 15	Assumption Day
October 5	Republic Day
November 1	All Saints' Day
December 1	Restoration Day
December 8	Immaculate Conception Day
December 25	Christmas Day

ARRIVAL & DEPARTURE

NEED TO KNOW

I'm on vacation [holiday]/business.	**Estou de férias/em negócios.** *ee • stawoo deh <u>feh</u> • ree • uhz/eng neh • <u>gaw</u> • see • yooz*
I'm going to…	**Vou para…** *vawoo <u>puh</u> • ruh…*
I'm staying at the… Hotel.	**Permaneço no hotel…** *pehr • muh • <u>neh</u> • soo noo aw • <u>tehl</u>…*

BORDER CONTROL

I'm just passing through.	**Estou só de passagem.** *ee • stawoo saw deh puh • <u>sah</u> • zheng*
I would like to declare…	**Queria declarar…** *keh • <u>ree</u> • uh deh • kluh • <u>rahr</u>…*
I have nothing to declare.	**Não tenhow nada a declarar.** *nohm <u>teh</u> • nyoo <u>nah</u> • duh uh deh • kluh • <u>rahr</u>*

YOU MAY SEE…

ALFÂNDEGA	customs
MERCADORIA SEM TAXAS	duty-free goods
ARTIGOS A DECLARAR	goods to declare
NADA A DECLARAR	nothing to declare
CONTROLE DE PASSAPORTES	passport control
POLÍCIA	police

YOU MAY HEAR...

O seu bilhete/passaporte.
oo sehoo bee•lyeht /pah•suh•pawrt

Your ticket/ passport, please.

Qual é o propósito de sua visita?
kwahl eh oo prau•paw•zee•too deh soo•uh vee•zee•tuh

What's the purpose of your visit?

Onde está a ficar?
aund ee•stah uh fee•kahr

Where are you staying?

Quanto tempo vai ficar?
kwuhn•too tehm•poo veye fee•kahr

How long are you staying?

Com quem está?
kohm keng ee•stah

Who are you with?

YOU MAY HEAR...

Tem alguma coisa a declarar?
teng ahl•goo•muh koy•zuh uh deh•kluh•rahr

Do you have anything to declare?

Tem de pagar direitos nisto.
teng deh puh•gahr dee•ray•tooz nee•stoo

You must pay duty on this.

Abra este saco, por favor.
ah•bruh eh•steh sah•koo poor fuh•vaur

Please open this bag.

MONEY

NEED TO KNOW

Where's...?	**Onde é...?**
	aund eh...
the ATM	**o multibanco**
	oo mool • tee • buhn • koo
the bank	**o banco**
	oo buhn • koo
the currency exchange office	**o câmbio**
	oo kuhm • bee • oo
What time does the bank open/close?	**A que horas é que o banco abre/ fecha?**
	uh keh aw • ruhz eh keh oo buhn • koo ah • breh/feh • shuh
I'd like to change dollars/pounds into euros/reais.	**Queria trocar dólares/libras em euros/reais.**
	keh • ree • uh troo • kahr daw • luhrz/ lee • bruhz eng ehoo • rooz/rree • eyez
I want to cash some traveler's checks [cheques].	**Quero cobrar cheques de viagem.**
	keh • roo koo • brahr sheh • kehz deh vee • ah • zseng

AT THE BANK

Can I exchange foreign currency/get a cash advance here?	**Posso trocar divisas estrangeiras/ obter dinheiro a crédito aqui?** _paw • soo troo • kahr dee • vee • zuhz_ _ee • struhn • zsay • ruhz au • btehr_ _dee • nyay • roo uh kreh • dee • too uh • kee_
What's the exchange rate?	**A como está o câmbio?** _uh koo • moo ee • stah oo kuhm • bee • oo_
How much commission do you charge?	**Quanto cobram de comissão?** _kwuhn • too kaw • brohm deh_ _koo • mee • sohm_
I think there's a mistake.	**Penso que há um erro.** _pehn • soo keh ah oong eh • rroo_
I've lost my traveler's checks [cheques].	**Perdi o meu livro de cheques.** _pehr • dee oo mehoo lee • vroo deh_ _sheh • kehz_
My card was lost.	**O meu cartão foi perdido.** _oo mehoo kuhr • tohm foy pehr • dee • thoo_
My credit card has been stolen.	**Roubaram-me o meu cartão de crédito.** _raw • bah • rohm meh oo mehoo_ _kuhr • tohm deh kreh • dee • too_

My credit card doesn't work.	**O meu cartão de crédito não funciona.**
	oo mehoo kuhr • tohm deh kreh • dee • too nohm foon • see • au • nuh
The ATM ate my card.	**A ATM ficou com o meu cartão.**
	uh ah • teh • ehm fee • kawoo kaum oo mehoo kuhr • tohm

For Numbers, see page 20.

YOU MAY SEE...

INSERIR O CARTÃO	insert card here
CANCELAR	cancel
APAGAR	clear
CONFIRMAR	enter
PIN	PIN
LEVANTAR FUNDOS	withdraw funds
DA CONTA CORRENTE	from checking [current] account
DA CONTA DE POUPANÇA	from savings account
RECIBO	receipt

CONVERSATION

Currency exchange offices **(Câmbio)** can be found
in most Portuguese tourist centers; they generally
stay open longer than banks, especially during the summer
season.
Travel agencies and hotels are other places where you can
exchange money, but the rate will not be as good. In heavy
tourist areas, you can also find currency exchange machines
on the streets. Of course, you should use caution when
exchanging money on the street, especially in cities.
Remember to take your passport with you when you want to
change money.

YOU MAY SEE...

In 2002 the currency in most EU countries, including
Portugal, changed to the **euro (€€)**, divided into 100
cêntimos (cents).

Coins: 1, 2, 5, 10, 20, 50 **cêntimos**; €1,2
Notes: €5, 10, 20, 50, 100, 200, 500

NEED TO KNOW

Hello.	**Olá.** _aw_ • lah
How are you?	**Como está?** _kau_ • moo ee • _stah_
Fine, thanks.	**Bem, obrigado** m/**obrigada** _f_. behm aw • bree • _gah_ • doo/ aw • bree • _gah_ • duh
Excuse me! (to get attention)	**Desculpe!** dehz • _kool_ • peh
Do you speak English?	**Fala inglês?** _fah_ • luh eeng • _lehz_
What's your name?	**Como se chama?** _kau_ • moo seh _shuh_ • muh
My name is…	**Chamo-me…** _shuh_ • moo meh…
Nice to meet you.	**Muito prazer.** _mooee_ • too pruh • _zehr_
Where are you from?	**De onde é?** deh aund eh
I'm from the U.S./ U.K.	**Sou dos Estados Unidos/da Inglaterra.** soh dooz ee • _stah_ • dooz oo • _nee_ • dooz/ duh eeng • luh • _teh_ • rruh
What do you do?	**O que é que faz?** oo kee eh keh fahz

I work for…	**Trabalho para…**
	truh • bah • lyoo puh • ruh…
I'm a student.	**Sou estudante.**
	sauoo ee • stoo • duhnt
I'm retired.	**Sou reformado** *m*/**reformada** *f.*
	soh reh • foor • mah • thoo/
	reh • foor • mah • thuh
Do you like…?	**Gosta de…?**
	gaw • stuh deh…
Goodbye.	**Adeus.**
	uh • deeooz
See you later.	**Até mais tarde.**
	uh • teh meyez tahrd

In Portuguese, there are a number of forms for 'you' (taking different verb forms): **tu** (singular) and **vós** (plural) are used when talking to relatives, close friends and children; **você** (singular) and **vocês** (plural) are used in all other cases. If in doubt as to which version to use, always use the polite version **você**/**vocês**.

LANGUAGE DIFFICULTIES

Do you speak English?	**Fala inglês?** *fah • luh eeng • lehz*
Does anyone here speak English?	**Há aqui alguém que fale inglês?** *ah uh • kee ahl • gehng keh fah • leh eeng • lehz*
I don't speak (much) Portuguese.	**Não falo (muito) português.** *nohm fah • loo (mooee • too) poor • too • gehz*
Could you speak more slowly?	**Pode falar mais devagar?** *pawd fuh • lahr meyez deh • vuh • gahr*
Could you repeat that?	**Pode repetir?** *pawd reh • peh • teer*
Excuse me? [Pardon?]	**Faça favor?** *fah • suh fuh • vaur*
What was that?	**Como disse?** *kau • moo dee • seh*
Could you spell it?	**Pode soletrar?** *pawd sau • leh • trahr*
Please write it down.	**Escreva, por favor.** *ee • screhv poor fuh • vaur*
Can you translate this for me?	**Pode traduzir-me isto?** *pawd truh • doo • zeer • meh ee • stoo*
What does this/that mean?	**O que significa isto/aquilo?** *oo keh sehg • nee • fee • kuh ee • stoo/ uh • kee • loo*
I understand.	**Compreendo.** *kaum • pree • ehn • doo*
I don't understand.	**Não compreendo.** *nohm kaum • pree • ehn • doo*
Do you understand?	**Entende?** *ehn • tehn • deh*

> **YOU MAY SEE...**
>
> **Falo só um pouco de Inglês.** I only speak a
> _fah • loo saw oong pau • koo deh eeng • lehz_ little English.
> **Nao falo Inglês.** I don't speak
> _nohm fah • loo eeng • lehz_ English.

MAKING FRIENDS

Hello.	**Olá.**
	aw • lah
Good morning.	**Bom dia.**
	bong dee • uh
Good afternoon.	**Boa tarde.**
	baw • uh tahrd
Good evening.	**Boa noite.**
	baw • uh noyt
My name is…	**Chamo-me…**
	shuh • moo meh…
What's your name?	**Como se chama?**
	kau • moo seh shuh • muh
I'd like to introduce you to…	**Gostaria de te apresentar ao/à…**
	goo • stuh • ree • uh deh the uh • preh • sehn • tahr ahoo/ah…
Nice to meet you.	**Muito prazer.**
	mooee • too preh • zehr
How are you?	**Como está?**
	kau • moo ee • stah
Fine, thanks.	**Bem, obrigado** _m_/**obrigada** _f._
	beng aw • bree • gah • doo/ aw • bree • gah • duh
And you?	**E o senhor** _m_/**a senhora** _f_?
	ee oo seh • nyaur/uh seh • nyau • ruh

In Portugal, a standard greeting is a handshake accompanied by direct eye contact and the appropriate greeting for the time of day. Once a closer relationship has developed, greetings become more personal: men may greet each other with a hug, and women kiss each other twice on the cheek starting with the right.

Note that anyone with a university degree is referred to as **Senhor Doutor** (literally, Mr. Doctor) if male or **Senhora Doutora** (Ms. Doctor) if female. Wait until invited before moving to a first-name basis.

TRAVEL TALK

I'm here…	**Estou aqui…**
	ee • stawoo uh • kee…
on business	**em negócios**
	eng neh • gaw • see • yooz
on vacation	**de férias**
[holiday]	*deh feh • ree • uhz*
studying	**a estudar**
	uh ee • stoo • dahr
I'm staying for…	**Fico por…**
	fee • koo poor…
I've been here…	**Eu já estive aqui…**
	ehoo zsah ee • stee • veh uh • kee…
a day	**um dia**
	oong dee • uh
a week	**uma semana**
	oo • muh seh • muh • nuh
a month	**um mês**
	oong mehz

Where are you from?	**De onde é?**
	deh aund eh
I'm from…	**Sou…**
	sawoo…

For Making Friends, see page 37.

PERSONAL

Who are you with?	**Com quem está?**
	kaun keng ee • <u>stah</u>
I'm on my own.	**Estou sozinho** *m*/**sozinha** *f.*
	ee • <u>stawoo</u> saw • <u>zee</u> • nyoo/
	saw • <u>zee</u> • nyuh
I'm with my…	**Estou com o meu** *m*/**a minha** *f…*
	ee • <u>stawoo</u> kaum oo mehoo/uh
	<u>mee</u> • nyuh…
husband/wife	**marido/mulher**
	muh • <u>ree</u> • thoo/moo • <u>lyehr</u>
boyfriend/	**namorado/namorada**
girlfriend	*nuh • moo • <u>rah</u> • thoo/nuh • moo • <u>rah</u> • thuh*
friend(s)	**amigo(s)** *m*/**amiga(s)** *f*
	uh • <u>mee</u> • goo(z)/uh • <u>mee</u> • guh(z)
colleague(s)	**colega(s)**
	koo • <u>leh</u> • guh(z)
When's your	**Quando faz anos?**
birthday?	*<u>kwuhn</u> • doo fahz <u>uh</u> • noos*
How old are you?	**Quantos anos tens?**
	<u>kwuhn</u> • tooz <u>uh</u> • noos tengz
I'm…	**Eu tenho…**
	ehoo <u>teh</u> • nyoo…
Are you married?	**É casado** *m*/**casada** *f?*
	eh kuh • <u>zah</u> • doo/kuh • <u>zah</u> • duh
I'm…	**Sou…/Estou…**
	sawoo/ee • <u>stawoo</u>…

single	**solteiro** m/**solteira** f
	saul • _tay_ • roo/saul • _tay_ • ruh
in a relationship	**num relacionamento**
	noong reh • luh • see • oo • nuh • _mehn_ • too
I'm…	**Sou…/Estou…**
	sawoo/ee • _stawoo_…
engaged	**comprometido**
	kaum • proo • meh • tee • doo
married	**casado** m/**casada** f
	kuh • _zah_ • doo/kuh • _zah_ • duh
divorced	**divorciado** m/**divorciada** f
	dee • voor • see • _ah_ • doo/
	dee • voor • see • _ah_ • duh
separated	**separado** m/**separada** f
	seh • puh • _rah_ • doo/seh • puh • _rah_ • duh
I'm widowed.	**Sou viúvo** m/**viúva** f.
	sau vee • _oo_ • voo/vee • _oo_ • vuh
Do you have children/ grandchildren?	**Tem filhos/netos?**
	teng fee • lyooz/neh • tooz

WORK & SCHOOL

What do you do?	**O que é que faz?**
	oo kee eh keh fahz
What are you studying?	**O que é que está a estudar?**
	oo kee eh keh ee • _stah_ uh ee • stoo • _dahr_
I'm studying…	**Estudo…**
	ee • _stoo_ • doo…
I work full time/ part time.	**Trabalho tempo integral/meio tempo.**
	truh • _bah_ • lyoo _tehm_ • poo een • teh • _grahl/_ _may_ • oo _tehm_ • poo
I'm between jobs.	**Estou entre empregos.**
	ee • _stawoo_ ehn • treh ehng • _preh_ • gooz

I'm unemployed.	**Estou desempregado.**
	ee • stawoo deh • zehm • preh • gah • doo.
I work at home.	**Trabalho em casa.**
	truh • <u>bah</u> • lyoo eng <u>kah</u> • zuh
Who do you work for?	**Para quem trabalha?**
	<u>puh</u> • ruh keng truh • <u>bah</u> • lyuh
I work for…	**Trabalho para…**
	truh • <u>bah</u> • lyoo puh • ruh…
Here's my business card.	**Aqui está meu cartão.**
	uh • <u>kee</u> ee • <u>stah</u> mehoo kuhr • <u>tohm</u>

For Social Media, see page 90.

WEATHER

What's the weather forecast?	**Quais são as previsões do tempo?**
	kweyez sohm uhz preh • vee • <u>zoings</u> thoo <u>tehm</u> • poo
What beautiful/ terrible weather!	**Que tempo tão lindo/ruim!**
	keh <u>tehm</u> • poo tohm <u>leen</u> • doo/rroo • <u>eeng</u>
It's cool/warm.	**Está fresco/calor.**
	ee • <u>stah</u> <u>frehs</u> • koo/kuh • <u>laur</u>
It's hot/cold.	**Está calor/frio.**
	ee • stah kuh • laur/free-oo.
It's rainy/sunny.	**Está um dia de chuva/sol.**
	ee • <u>stah</u> oong <u>dee</u> • uh deh <u>shoo</u> • vuh/ sawl
It's snowy/icy.	**Está um dia de neve/com gelo.**
	ee • <u>stah</u> oong <u>dee</u> • uh deh nehv/kaum zseh • loo
Do I need a jacket/ an umbrella?	**Preciso de um casaco/guarda-chuva?**
	preh • <u>see</u> • zoo deh oong kuh • <u>zah</u> • koo/ goo • ahr • <u>dah</u> <u>shoo</u> • vuh

ON THE WAY

GETTING AROUND 44

PLACES TO STAY 71

COMMUNICATIONS 87

SIGHTSEEING 97

GETTING AROUND

NEED TO KNOW

How do I get to the city center?	**Como é que vou para o centro da cidade?** _kau_ • moo eh keh vawoo _puh_ • ruh oo sehn • troo duh see • _dahd_
Where's…?	**Onde é…?** _aund_ _eh_…
the airport	**o aeroporto** oo uh • eh • rau • _paur_ • too
the train station [the railway station]	**a estação de caminho de ferro** uh ee • stuh • _sohm_ deh kuh • _mee_ • nyoo deh _feh_ • rroo
the bus station	**a estação de camionetas** uh ee • stuh • _sohm_ deh kah • meeoo • _neh_ • tuhz
the metro [underground] station	**a estação de metro** uh ee • stuh • _sohm_ deh meh • troo
How far is it?	**A que distância fica?** uh keh dee • _stuhn_ • see • uh _fee_ • kuh
Where can I buy tickets?	**Onde posso comprar bilhetes?** aund _paw_ • soo kaum • _prahr_ bee • _lyehtz_
A one-way/return-trip ticket to…	**Um bilhete de ida/de ida e volta para…** oong bee • _lyeht_ deh ee • thuh/deh ee • thuh ee _vaul_ • tuh puh • ruh…

How much?	**Quanto custa?**
	kwuhn • too _koo_ • stuh
Are there any discounts?	**Há descontos?**
	ah dehs • caun • tooz
Which…?	**Qual…?**
	kwahl…
gate	**porta**
	port • uh
line	**linha**
	lee • nyuh
platform	**plataforma**
	plah • tuh • fawr • muh
Where can I get a taxi?	**Onde posso apanhar um táxi?**
	aund paw • soo uh • puh • nyar oong tahk • see
Please take me to this address.	**Leve-me a esta morada.**
	leh • veh • meh uh eh • stuh maw • rah • duh
Where can I rent a car?	**Onde posso alugar um carro?**
	aund paw • soo uh • loo • gahr oong kah • rroo
Could I have a map?	**Pode dar-me um mapa?**
	pawd dahr • meh oong mah • puh

Portugal is well-served by public transport in general, with good rail and bus networks, especially between the bigger cities. Transport to smaller villages is best served by car and the roads generally provide good driving conditions.

TICKETS

When's...to...?	**A que horas é...para...?**
	uh kee <u>aw</u> • ruhz eh...<u>puh</u> • ruh...
the (first) bus	**a (primeira) camioneta**
	uh (pree • <u>may</u> • ruh)
	kah • meeoo • <u>neh</u> • tuh
the (next) flight	**o (próximo) vôo**
	oo (<u>praw</u> • see • moo) <u>vau</u> • oo
the (last) train	**o (último) comboio**
	oo (<u>ool</u> • tee • moo) kaum • <u>baw</u> • eeoo
Where can I buy tickets?	**Onde posso comprar bilhetes?**
	aund <u>paw</u> • soo kaum • <u>prahr</u> bee • <u>lyehtz</u>
One/Two ticket(s), please.	**Um bilhete/Dois bilhetes, se faz favor.**
	oong bee • <u>lyeht</u>/doyz bee • <u>lyehtz</u> seh fahz
	fuh • <u>vaur</u>
For today/tomorrow.	**Para hoje/amanhã.**
	puh • ruh auzseh/uh • muh • <u>nyuh</u>
A(n)...ticket.	**Um bilhete...**
	oong bee • <u>lyeht</u>...
one-way	**de ida**
	deh <u>ee</u> • thuh
return-trip	**de ida e volta**
	deh <u>ee</u> • thuh ee <u>vaul</u> • tuh

first-class	**em primeira classe**
business class	*eng pree • may • ruh klah • she*
economy class	**em classe económica**
	eng klah • seh eh • koo • naw • mee • kuh
How much?	**Quanto custa?**
	kwuhn • too koo • stuh
Is there a discount for…?	**Há desconto para…?**
	ah dehs • kaum • too puh • ruh…
children	**crianças**
	kree • uhn • suhz
students	**estudantes**
	ee • stoo • duhnts
senior citizens	**os reformados**
	ooz reh • faur • mah • dooz
tourists	**turistas**
	too • ree • stuhz
The express bus/ express train, please.	**A camioneta expresso/o comboio expresso, por favor.**
	uh kah • meeoo • neh • tuh/oo kaum • baw • eeoo ees • preh • soo, poor fuh • vaur
The local bus/train, please	**A camioneta/o comboio local, por favor.**
	uh kah • meeoo • neh • tuh/oo kaum • baw • eeoo loo • kahl, poor fuh • vaur
I have an e-ticket.	**Eu tenho um bilhete electrónico.**
	ehoo teh • nyoo oong bee • lyeht ee • lek • tro • nee • kuh
Can I buy a ticket on the bus/train?	**Posso comprar o bilhete na camioneta/no comboio?**
	paw • soo kaum • prahr oo bee • lyeht nuh kah • mee • oo • neh • tuh/ noo kaum • baw • ee • oo

Do I have to stamp the ticket before boarding?	**Tenho de carimbar o bilhete antes de embarcar?** *teh • nyoo deh kuh • reem • bahr oo bee • lyeht uhnts deh ehm • buhr • kahr*
How long is this ticket valid?	**Até quando é que este bilhete é válido?** *uh • teh kwuhn doo eh keh ehst bee • lyeht eh vah • lee • doo*
Can I return on the same ticket?	**Posso voltar com o mesmo bilhete?** *paw • soo vaul • tuhr kaum oo mehz • moo bee • lyeht*
I'd like to…my reservation.	**Queria…a minha reserva.** *keh • ree • uh…uh mee • nyuh reh • zehr • vuh*
cancel	**cancelar** *kuhn • seh • lahr*
change	**mudar** *moo • dahr*
confirm	**confirmar** *kaum • feer • mahr*

For Days, see page 24.

AIRPORT TRANSFER

How much is a taxi to the airport?	**Quanto custa um táxi para o aeroporto?** *kwuhn • too koo • stuh oong tahk • see puh • ruh oo uh • eh • rau • paur • too*
To…Airport, please.	**Ao aeroporto de…, por favor.** *ahoo uh • eh • rau • paur • too deh…poor fuh • vaur*
My airline is…	**A minha linha aérea é…** *uh mee • nyuh lee • nyuh ah • ehr • ee • uh eh…*
My flight leaves at…	**O meu vôo parte às…** *oo meeoo vau • oo pahr • teh ahz…*

I'm in a hurry.	**Estou com pressa.**
	ee • <u>stawoo</u> kaum <u>preh</u> • suh
Can you take an alternate route?	**Pode tomar um caminho alternativo?**
	pawd too • <u>mahr oong kuh</u> • <u>mee</u> • <u>nyoo</u> ahl • tehr • <u>nah</u> • tee • vuh
Can you drive faster/ slower?	**Pode guiar mais rápido/ devagar?**
	pawd gee • <u>ahr</u> meyez <u>rah</u> • pee • thoo/ deh • vuh • <u>gahr</u>

For Time, see page 23.

YOU MAY HEAR...

Que linha aérea voam?	What airline are you flying?
keh <u>lee</u> • nyuh ah • <u>eh</u> • ree • uh <u>vau</u> • ohm	
Doméstico ou internacional?	Domestic or international?
thoo • <u>meh</u> • stee • koo awoo een • tehr • <u>nuh</u> • seeoo • nahl	
Que terminal?	What terminal?
keh tehr • mee • <u>nahl</u>	

There are international airports in Lisbon and Porto, located on the outskirts of the cities. Tap Air Portugal is the national airline and it operates a daily service between Lisbon, Porto, Faro, Madeira and the Azores islands.

YOU MAY SEE...

CHEGADAS	arrivals
PARTIDAS	departures
ENTREGA DE BAGAGEM	baggage claim
VÔOS DOMÉSTICOS	domestic flights
VÔOS INTERNACIONAIS	international flights
REGISTO	check-in desk
REGISTO BILHETE ELECTRÓNICO	e-ticket check-in
PORTÕES DE PARTIDA	departure gates

CHECKING IN

Where is the check-in counter?	**Onde é o check in?**
	aund eh oo check in
My name is...	**Chamo-me...**
	shuh • moo meh...
I'm going to...	**Vou para...**
	vauoo puh • ruh...
I have...	**Tenho...**
	teh • nyoo...
one suitcase	**uma mala**
	oo • muh mah • luh
two suitcases	**duas malas**
	thoo • uhz mah • luhs
one piece of hand luggage	**uma bagagem de mão**
	oo • muh buh • gah • geng deh mohm
How much luggage is allowed?	**Quantas bagagens são permitidas?**
	kwuhn • tuhz buh • gah • zsengs sohm pehr • mee • tee • thuhs

YOU MAY HEAR...

Próximo!
praw • see • moo

Next!

O seu bilhete/passaporte, faz favor.
*oo sehoo bee • lyet/pah • suh • pawrt fahz
fuh • vaur*

Your ticket/
passport,
please.

Tem bagagem para despachar?
*teng buh • gah • zseng puh • ruh
dehs • puh • shahr*

Are you
checking any
luggage?

Tem excesso de peso na sua bagagem.
*teng eh • zeh • soo deh peh • zoo nuh
soo • uh buh • gah • zseng*

You have
excess baggage.

**Isso é demasiado volumoso para
bagagem de mão.**
*ee • soo eh deh • muh • zee • ah • thoo
vaw • loo • mau • zoo
puh • ruh buh • gah • zseng deh mohm*

That's too large
for a carry-on
[to carry on
board].

**Foi o senhor m/a senhora f quem fez
as malas?**
*foy oo see • nyaur/ uh see • nyau • ruh
keng fehz uhs mah • luhs*

Did you pack
these bags
yourself?

**Alguém lhe deu alguma coisa para
transportar?**
*ahl • geng lyeh dehoo ahl • goo • muh
coy • zuh puh • ruh truhns • pawr • tahr*

Did anyone give
you anything to
carry?

Tire tudo dos bolsos.
tee • reh too • thoo dooz bawl • sooz

Empty your
pockets.

Tire os seus sapatos.
tee • reh ooz sehooz suh • pah • tooz

Take off your
shoes.

Estamos a embarcar o vôo...
*ee • stuh • mooz uh eng • buhr • kahr oo
vau • oo...*

Now boarding
flight...

Is that pounds or kilos?	**Isso está em libras ou quilos?** *ee • soo ee • stah eng lee • bruhz awoo kee • laes*
Which terminal/gate does flight…leave from?	**Qual é o terminal para o vôo/a porta do vôo para…?** *kwahl eh oo tehr • mee • <u>nahl puh</u> • <u>ruh oo</u> <u>vau</u> • oo/uh <u>pawr</u> • tuhz thoo <u>vau</u> • oo <u>puh</u> • ruh…*
I'd like a window/ an aisle seat.	**Queria um lugar à janela/na coxia.** *keh • <u>ree</u> • uh oong loo • <u>gahr</u> ah zsuh • <u>neh</u> • luh/nuh kau • sheeuh*
When do we leave/ arrive?	**Quando vamos partir/chegar?** *<u>kwuhn</u> • doo <u>vuh</u> • mooz puhr • <u>teer</u>/ shee • <u>gahr</u>*
Is flight…delayed?	**Há atraso no vôo…?** *ah uh • <u>trah</u> • zoo noo <u>vau</u> • oo…*
How late will it be?	**Qual é o atraso?** *kwahl eh oo uh • <u>trah</u> • zoo*

For Time, see page 23.

LUGGAGE

Where is/are…?	**Onde é/são…?** *aund eh/sohm…*
the luggage trolleys	**os carrinhos** *ooz kuh • <u>rree</u> • nyos*
the luggage lockers	**os cacifos de bagagem** *ooz kuh • <u>see</u> • fooz deh buh • <u>gah</u> • zseng*
the baggage claim	**o depósito de bagagem** *oo deh • <u>paw</u> • zee • too deh buh • <u>gah</u> • zseng*
My luggage has been lost.	**Perdi a minha bagagem.** *pehr • <u>dee</u> uh <u>mee</u> • nyuh buh • <u>gah</u> • zseng*

My luggage has been stolen.	**Roubaram a minha bagagem.**
	raw • <u>bah</u> • rohm uh <u>mee</u> • nyuh buh • <u>gah</u> • zseng
My suitcase was damaged.	**A minha mala foi danificada.**
	uh <u>mee</u> • nyuh mah • luh foy deh • nee • fee • <u>kah</u> • thuh

For Police, see page 144.

FINDING YOUR WAY

Where is/are…?	**Onde é/são…?**
	aund eh/sohm
the currency exchange office	**o câmbio**
	oo <u>kuhm</u> • bee • oo
the car hire	**o aluguer de carros**
	oo uh • loo • <u>gehr</u> deh <u>kah</u> • rrooz
the exit	**a saída**
	uh suh • <u>ee</u> • thuh
the taxis	**os táxis**
	ooz <u>tahk</u> • seez
Is there…into town?	**Há…para o centro?**
	ah…<u>puh</u> • ruh oo <u>sehn</u> • troo
a bus	**um autocarro**
	oong ahoo • too • <u>kah</u> • rroo
a train	**um comboio**
	oong kaum • <u>boy</u> • oo
a metro [underground]	**um metro**
	oong <u>meh</u> • troo

For Asking Directions, see page 66.

TRAIN

Where's the nearest train station?	**Onde está a estação de comboios mais próxima?**
	aund ee • stah uh ee • stuh • sohm deh kaum • boy • ooz meyez praw • see • muh
How far is it?	**A que distância fica?**
	uh keh dee • stuhn • see • uh fee • kuh
Where is/are...?	**Onde está/são...?**
	aund ee • stah/sohm...
the ticket office	**a bilheteira**
	uh bee • lyeht • ay • ree • uh
the information desk	**as informações**
	uhz een • foor • muh • soingz
the luggage lockers	**os cacifos de bagagem**
	ooz kuh • see • fooz deh buh • gah • zseng
the platforms	**as linhas**
	uhz lee • nyuhz
Could I have a schedule [timetable], please?	**Queria um horário, se faz favor.**
	keh • ree • uh oong aw • rah • ree • oo seh fahz fuh • vaur

The Portuguese railway, **Caminhos de Ferro Portugueses (C.P.),** handles almost all train services in Portugal and totals 1,771 miles of track. Tickets can be purchased and reservations can be made through travel agencies and at train stations. You may also purchase your ticket on the train and at various **multibancos** (ATMs). Check out the various special prices and travel cards available (for 7, 14 and 21 days). Note also that rates are cheaper on 'Blue Days' (**dias azuis**), and a 'Gold Card' is available for people over 65.

How long is the trip?	**Quanto tempo demora a viagem?**
	kwuhn • too <u>tehm</u> • poo deh • maw • ruh uh vee • <u>ah</u> • zseng
Is it a direct train?	**É um comboio directo?**
	eh oong kaum • baw • eeoo dee • reh • too
Do I have to change trains?	**Tenho de mudar de comboio?**
	<u>teh</u> • nyoo deh moo • <u>dahr</u> deh kaum • <u>boy</u> • oo
Is the train on time?	**O comboio chega a horas?**
	oo kaum • baw • eeoo shee • gah uh aw • ruhz

YOU MAY SEE...

PARA AS LINHAS	to the platforms
INFORMAÇÕES	information
RESERVAS	reservations
SALA DE ESPERA	waiting room
CHEGADAS	arrivals
PARTIDAS	departures

DEPARTURES

Which track [platform] for the train to...?	**De que linha parte o comboio para...?**
	deh keh lee • nyuh pahrt oo kaum • <u>boy</u> • oo puh • ruh...
Is this the track [platform] to...?	**É daqui que parte o comboio para...?**
	eh duh • <u>kee</u> keh pahrt oo kaum • <u>boy</u> • oo puh • ruh...
Where is track [platform]...?	**Onde é a linha...?**
	aund eh uh <u>lee</u> • nyuh...

Where do I change for...?	**Onde é que mudo para...?**
	aund eh keh <u>moo</u>•thoo puh•ruh...

For Communications, see page 87.

ON BOARD

Is this seat taken?	**Este lugar está ocupado?**
	ehst loo•<u>gahr</u> ee•<u>stah</u>
	aw•koo•<u>pah</u>•thoo
Can I sit here/ open the window?	**Posso sentar-me aqui/abrir a janela?**
	paw•soo sehn•tahr•meh uh•kee/
	ah•breer uh zsuh•neh•luh
That's my seat.	**Esse é o meu lugar.**
	<u>eh</u>•seh eh oo mehoo loo•<u>gahr</u>
Here's my reservation.	**Aqui está a minha reserva.**
	uh•kee ee•stah uh mee•nyuh
	reh•zehr•vuh

For Tickets, see page 46.

BUS

Where's the bus station?	**Onde é a estação de camionetas?**
	aund eh uh ee•stuh•<u>sohm</u> deh
	<u>kah</u>•meeoo•<u>neh</u>•tuhz

In Lisbon, a tram also operates along some routes. Stops are indicated by large signs marked **paragem** (stop). The most popular route is the No.28 that goes from barrio Alto to Alfama and the castle. Most trams are entered from the front where you can buy a ticket from the driver.

How far is it?	**A que distância fica?**
	uh keh dee • stuhn • see • uh fee • kuh
How do I get to…?	**Como se vai para…?**
	kau • moo seh veye puh • ruh…
Does the bus [coach] stop at…?	**A camioneta pára em…?**
	uhkah • myoo • neh • tuh pah • ruh eng…
Could you tell me when to get off?	**Pode-me dizer quando eu devo sair?**
	paw • deh meh dee • zehr kwuhn • doo deh • voo suh • eer
Do I have to change buses?	**Tenho de mudar de autocarro?**
	teh • nyoo deh moo • dahr deh ahoo • too • kah • rroo
Stop here, please!	**Pare aqui, por favor!**
	pah • reh uh • kee poor fuh • vaur

YOU MAY HEAR…

Todos a bordo!
toah • thooz uh baur • thoo

All aboard!

Bilhetes, por favor.
bee • lyehtz poor fuh • vaur

Tickets, please.

Tem de mudar em…
teng deh moo • dahr eng…

You have to change at…

A próxima paragem…
uh praw • see • muh puh • rah • zseng…

Next stop…

In Portugal, intercity bus services are frequent
and cover most of the country. Some buses are run by the
Portuguese Transport Company, **Rodoviária Nacional (R.N.)**,
while others are privately owned.

METRO

Where's the nearest metro [underground] station?	**Onde é a estação de metro mais próxima?** *aund eh uh ee • stuh • <u>sohm</u> deh <u>meh</u> • troo meyez <u>praw</u> • see • muh*
Could I have a map of the subway [underground], please?	**Pode dar-me um mapa do metro, por favor.** *pawd <u>dahr</u> • meh oong <u>mah</u> • puh thoo <u>meh</u> • troo poor fuh • <u>vaur</u>*
Which line for…?	**Qual é a linha para…?** *kwahl eh uh <u>lee</u> • nyuh <u>puh</u> • ruh…*
Do I have to transfer [change]?	**Tenho que transferir?** *teh • nyoo keh truhns • feh • <u>reer</u>*
Is this the metro to…?	**Este comboio vai para…?** *ehst kaum • <u>boy</u> • oo veye <u>puh</u> • ruh…*
Where are we?	**Onde estamos?** *aund ee • <u>stuh</u> • mooz*

The subway system in Lisbon has four main lines
and operates at forty-four stations throughout metropolitan
Lisbon, including regular services to and from the airport.
Buy a **senha**, a single flat-rate ticket, or a booklet of ten
tickets at ticket offices or machines.

YOU MAY SEE...

PARAGEM DE AUTOCARROS	bus stop
ENTRADA/SAÍDA	enter/exit
MARQUE O SEU BILHETE	stamp your ticket
STOP	request stop

BOAT & FERRY

When is the ferry to...?	**Quando é o barco para...?**
	kwuhn • doo eh oo <u>bahr</u> • koo puh • ruh...
Can I take my car?	**Posso levar o meu carro?**
	paw • soo loo • <u>vahr</u> oo mehoo <u>kah</u> • rroo
What time is the next sailing?	**A que horas parte o próximo barco?**
	au qeh aw • ruhz pahr • teh oo praw • see • moo bahr • koo
Can I book a seat/cabin?	**Posso reservar um lugar/uma cabina?**
	paw • soo reh • zehr • vuhr oong loo • gahr/ oo • muh kuh • bee • nuh
How long is the crossing?	**Quanto tempo demora a viagem?**
	kwuhn • too tehm • poo deh • maw • ruh uh vee • ah • zseng

YOU MAY SEE...

BARCO SALVA-VIDAS	life boat
COLETE DE SALVAÇÃO	life jacket

TAXI

Where can I get a taxi?	**Onde posso apanhar um táxi?**
	aund <u>paw</u> • soo uh • puh • <u>nyahr</u> oong <u>tahk</u> • see
Can you send a taxi?	**Pode enviar um táxi?**
	pawd ehn • vee • ahr oong tahk • see
I'd like a taxi now/ for tomorrow at…	**Queria um táxi agora/amanhã às…**
	keh • <u>ree</u> • uh oong <u>tahk</u> • see uh • <u>gaw</u> • ruh/uh • muh • <u>nyuh</u> ahz…
Pick me up at… (place/time)	**Apanhe-me no/às…**
	uh • <u>puh</u> • nyeh • meh noo/ahz…
I'm going to…	**Vou para…**
	<u>vau</u> • oo <u>puh</u> • ruh…
this address	**esta morada**
	<u>eh</u> • stuh maw • <u>rah</u> • duh
the airport	**o aeroporto**
	oo uh • eh • rau • <u>paur</u> • too
the train [railway] station	**à estação dos comboios**
	ah ee • stuh • <u>sohm</u> dooz kaum • <u>boy</u> • ooz
I'm late.	**Estou atrasado m/atrasada f.**
	ee • <u>stawoo</u> uh • truh • <u>zah</u> • thoo/ uh • truh • <u>zah</u> • thuh

i

Taxis in Portugal are cream colored or black with a green roof.
Rural taxis, including those at airports, are marked 'A' (**aluguer**) and are usually without a meter, but follow a standard-fare table. They are easily hailed in much of Lisbon, and fares are generally cheap.

Can you drive faster/ slower?	**Pode guiar mais rápido/ devagar?**
	pawd gee•ahr meyez rrah•pee•thoo/ deh•vuh•gahr
Stop/Wait here.	**Pare/Espere aqui.**
	pah•reh/ee•speh•reh uh•kee
How much?	**Quanto é?**
	kwuhn•too eh
You said it would cost...euros.	**Disse que ia custar...euros.**
	thee•seh keh ee•uh koo•stahr... ehoo•rooz
A receipt, please.	**Um recibo, se faz favor.**
	oong reh•see•boo seh fahz fuh•vaur
Keep the change.	**Guarde o troco.**
	goo•ahr•deh oo trau•koo

YOU MAY HEAR...

Para donde?	Where to?
puh·ruh thaun·deh	
Qual é a morada [direção]?	What's the
kwahl eh uh maw·rah·duh [dee·reh·sohm]	address?
Há uma taxa extra nocturna/ de aeroporto.	There's a nighttime/
ah oo•muh tah•shuh ehs•truh naw•toor•nuh/ deh uh•eh•rau•paur•too	airport surcharge.

BICYCLE & MOTORBIKE

Where can I rent...?	**Onde posso alugar...?**
	aund <u>paw</u> • soo uh • loo • <u>gahr</u>...
a 3-/10-speed bicycle	**uma bicicleta de trêz/ dez velocidades**
	<u>oo</u> • muh bee • see • <u>kleh</u> • tuh deh trehz/ dehz veh • <u>law</u> • see • <u>dah</u> • dehz
a moped	**uma lambreta**
	<u>oo</u> • muh luhm • <u>breh</u> • tuh
a motorcycle	**uma motocicleta**
	<u>oo</u> • muh maw • taw • see • <u>kleh</u> • tuh
How much per day/ week?	**Quanto custa por dia/semana?**
	<u>kwuhn</u> • too <u>koo</u> • stuh poor <u>deeuh</u>/ seh<u>muhnuh</u>
Can I have a helmet?	**Posso ter uma capacete?**
	<u>paw</u> • soo tehr <u>oo</u> • muh kuhpuh<u>seh</u>the
Can I have a lock?	**Posso ter uma corrente?**
	<u>paw</u> • soo tehr <u>oo</u> • muh koo<u>rrehnt</u>

CAR HIRE

Where can I rent a car?	**Onde posso alugar um carro?**
	aund <u>paw</u> • soo uh • loo • <u>gahr</u> oong <u>kah</u> • rroo
I'd like to rent…	**Queria alugar…**
	keh • <u>ree</u> • uh uh • loo • <u>gahr</u>…
a cheap/small car	**um carro barato/pequeno**
	oong kah • rroo buh • rah • too/ peh • keh • noo
a 2-/4-door car	**um carro de duas/quatro portas**
	oong <u>kah</u> • rroo deh <u>thoo</u> • uhz/<u>kwah</u> • troo <u>pawr</u> • tuhz

YOU MAY HEAR…

Tem uma carta de condução internacional?	Do you have an international driver's license?
teng <u>oo</u> • muh <u>kahr</u> • tuh deh kaum • doo • <u>sohm</u> een • tehr • nuh • see • oo • <u>nahl</u>	
O seu passaporte, por favor.	Your passport, please.
oo sehoo pah • suh • <u>pawr</u> • teh poor fuh • <u>vaur</u>	
Quer seguro?	Do you want insurance?
kehr seh • <u>goo</u> • roo	
É preciso deixar um sinal de…	There is a deposit of…
eh preh • <u>see</u> • zoo day • <u>shahr</u> oong see • <u>nahl</u> deh…	
Assine aqui, se faz favor.	Please sign here.
uh • <u>see</u> • neh uh • <u>kee</u> seh fahz fuh • <u>vaur</u>	

a(n) automatic/ manual	**um carro automático/de mudanças** *oong kah • rro awoo • too • mah • tee • koo/ deh moo • thuhn • suhz*
a car with air conditioning	**um carro com ar condicionado** *oong kah • rro kaum ahr kawn • dee • seeoo • nah • thoo*
a car seat	**um assento de carro de bebé** *oong uh • sehn • too deh kah • rro deh beh • beh*
How much…	**Quanto é…?** *kwuhn • too eh…*
per day/week	**por dia/semana** *poor dee • uh/seh • muh • nuh*
per kilometer	**por quilómetro** *poor kee • law • meh • troo*
for unlimited mileage	**com quilometragem ilimitada** *kaum kee • lae • meh • trah • zseng ee • lee • mee • tah • thuh*
with insurance	**com seguro** *kaum seh • goo • roo*
Are there any discounts?	**Há descontos?** *ah dehs • kaum • tooz*

For Days, see page 24.

YOU MAY SEE…

NORMAL	regular
SUPER	premium [super]
GASÓLEO [DIESEL]	diesel

FUEL STATION

Where's the next fuel station?	**Onde é a bomba de gasolina mais próxima?**
	aund eh uh <u>baum</u> • buh deh guh • zoo • <u>lee</u> • nuh meyez <u>praw</u> • see • muh
Fill it up, please.	**Encha o depósito, se faz favor.**
	<u>ehn</u> • shuh oo deh • <u>paw</u> • zee • too seh fahz fuh • <u>vaur</u>
...liters, please.	**...litros, se faz favor.**
	...<u>lee</u> • trooz seh fahz fuh • <u>vaur</u>
I'll pay in cash/by credit card.	**Pago com dinheiro/com o cartão de crédito.**
	<u>pah</u> • goo kaum dee<u>nyay</u>roo/kaum oo kuhr<u>tohm</u> deh <u>kreh</u>deetoo

For Numbers, see page 20.

A word of caution: outside of major cities, Portugal is mostly mountainous terrain with small, narrow, two-way streets. Overtaking slow moving traffic on the left is permissible, but use caution.
At night, when on these unlit winding roads, flash your high beams before every turn to let any oncoming cars on the opposite side know that there's a car around the bend.

ASKING DIRECTIONS

Is this the right road to…?	**Esta é a estrada que vai para…?** *eh • stuh eh uh ee • strah • duh keh veye puh • ruh…*
How far is it to…?	**A que distância fica…?** *uh keh dee • stuhn • see • uh fee • kuh…*
Where's…?	**Onde fica…?** *aund fee • kuh…*
…Street	**a rua…** *uh rroo • uh…*
this address	**esta morada** *eh • stuh maw • rah • duh*
the highway [motorway]	**a auto-estrada** *uh ahoo • taw • strah • duh*
Can you show me on the map?	**Pode-me indicar no mapa?** *pawd meh een • dee • kahr noo mah • puh*
I'm lost.	**Estou perdido** m/**perdida** f. *ee • stawoo pehr • dee • doo/pehr • dee • duh*

PARKING

Can I park here?	**Posso estacionar aqui?** *paw • soo ee • stuh • seeoo • nahr uh • kee*
Where is the nearest parking garage?	**Onde fica a garagem mais próxima?** *aund fee • kuh uh guh • rah • zseng meyez praw • see • muh*
Where is the nearest parking lot [car park]?	**Onde fica o parque de estacionamento mais próximo?** *aund fee • kuh oo pahr • keh deh ee • stuh • seeawn • uh • mehn • too meyez praw • see • moo*

YOU MAY HEAR...

sempre em frente _sehm • preh eng frehn • teh_	straight ahead
à esquerda _ah ee • skehr • duh_	on the left
à direita _ah dee • ray • tuh_	on the right
depois de/ao dobrar da esquina _deh • poyz deh/ahoo doo • brahr duh ees • kee • nuh_	on/around the corner
em frente de _eng frehn • teh deh_	opposite
por trás de _poor trahz deh_	behind
a seguir ao _m_/à _f_ _uh seh • geer ahoo/ah_	next to
depois do _m_/da _f_ _deh • poyz thoo/duh_	after
norte/sul _nawrt/sool_	north/south
leste/oeste _lehs • the/aw • ehs • teh_	east/west
no semáforo _noo seh • mah • fau • roo_	at the traffic light
no cruzamento _noo croo • zuh • mehn • too_	at the intersection

Where's the parking meter?	**Onde está o parquímetro?** _aund ee • stah oo pahr • kee • meh • troo_

How much?	**Quanto é...?**
	kwuhn • too eh...
per hour	**por hora**
	poor <u>aw</u> • ruh
per day	**por dia**
	poor <u>dee</u> • uh
overnight	**só uma noite**
	saw <u>oo</u> • muh noyt

BREAKDOWN & REPAIR

My car broke down/ won't start.	**O meu carro avariou/O motor não pega.**
	oo mehoo <u>kah</u> • rroo uh • vuh • ree • <u>awoo</u>/ oo moo • <u>taur</u> nohm <u>peh</u> • guh
Can you fix it (today)?	**Pode consertá-lo (hoje)?**
	pawd kaum • sehr • <u>tah</u> • loo (oyzseh)
When will it be ready?	**Quando estará pronto?**
	<u>kwuhn</u> • doo ee • stuh • <u>rah praun</u> • too

ⓘ

Metered parking is common in most towns. During business hours there is a 90- or 120-minute parking limit; stick to it or you can get fined. Certain cities have blue zones—streets marked with blue-colored signs where you can pay to park. A ticket machine is usually located in the middle of the block and accepts parking tokens. These parking tokens are available from the police or the Portuguese Motoring Organization (ACP). To park in this zone, purchase a ticket and display it in your windshield.

YOU MAY SEE...

Road Signs in Portugal are 'universal,' that is, there is no language associated with them. Here are the most common signs with the English explanation beside them:

 proibido ultrapassar — do not pass

 sentido proibido — no entry

 estacionamento proibido — no parking

 limite de velocidade — speed limit

 paragem obrigatória — stop

 final de faixa — lane ends

 dar prioridade — yield

How much is it?	**Quanto custa?**
	kwuhn • too koo • stuh
I have a puncture/ flat tyre (tire).	**Tenho um furo/pneu sem ar.**
	teh • nyoo oong foo • roo/pnehoo seng ahr

ACCIDENTS

There has been an accident.	**Houve um acidente.** *auoov oong uh • see • dehnt*
Call an ambulance.	**Chame uma ambulância.** *shuh • meh oo • muh* *uhm • boo • luhn • see • uh*
Call the police.	**Chame a polícia.** *shuh • meh uh poo • lee • see • uh*

For Police, see page 144.

The Potuguese police can be identified by their blue uniforms and are generally helful and friendly. They often speak a little English too.
Traffic police wear red armbands with a silver letter **T** (for **Trânsito**, or traffic) on a red background, a white helmet and white gloves.
On highways, traffic is controlled by the Guardia Nacional Republicana (GNR) in white and red or white and blue cars, or on motorcycles.

PLACES TO STAY

NEED TO KNOW

Can you recommend a hotel?	**Pode recomendar-me um hotel?** *pawd reh • kaw • mehn • dahr • meh oong aw • tehl*
I have a reservation.	**Tenho uma reserva.** *teh • nyoo oo • muh reh • zehr • vuh*
My name is…	**Chamo-me…** *shuh • moo • meh…*
Do you have a room…?	**Tem um quarto…?** *teng oong kwahr • too…*
for one/two	**para um/dois** *puh • ruh oong/doyz*
with a bathroom	**com quarto de banho** *kaum kwahr • too deh buh • nyoo*
with air conditioning	**com ar condicionado** *kaum ar kawn • dee • seeoo • nah • thoo*
For…	**Para…** *puh • ruh…*
tonight	**hoje à noite** *auzseh ah noyt*
two nights	**duas noites** *thoo • uhz noytz*
one week	**uma semana** *oo • muh seh • muh • nuh*
How much is it?	**Quanto custa?** *kwuhn • too koo • stuh*

Do you have anything cheaper?	**Há mais barato?** *ah meyez buh • rah • too*
What time is check-out?	**A que horas temos de deixar o quarto?** *uh kee aw • ruhz teh • mooz deh thay • shahr oo kwahr • too*
Can I leave this in the safe?	**Posso deixar isto no cofre?** *paw • soo thay • shahr ee • stoo noo kaw • freh*
Can I leave my bags?	**Posso deixar a minha bagagem?** *paw • soo day • shahr uh mee • nyuh buh • gah • geng*
Can I have the bill/a receipt?	**Pode dar-me a conta/uma factura?** *pawd dahr • meh uh kaum • tuh/oo • muh fah • too • ruh*
I'll pay in cash/by credit card.	**Pago com dinheiro/com o cartão de crédito.** *pah • goo kaum dee • nyay • roo/ kaum oo kuhr • tohm deh kreh • dee • too*

SOMEWHERE TO STAY

Can you recommend…?	**Pode recomendar-me…?** *pawd reh • kaw • mehn • dahr • meh*
a hotel	**um hotel** *oong aw • tehl*
a hostel	**uma pousada** *oo • muh pawoo • zah • thuh*
a campsite	**um parque de campismo** *oong pahr • keh deh kuhm • peez • moo*
a bed and breakfast	**uma residencial** *oo • muh reh • zee • dehn • see • ahl*

What is it near?	**É perto de quê?**
	eh pehr • too deh keh
How do I get there?	**Como se vai para lá?**
	kau • moo seh veye puh • ruh lah

AT THE HOTEL

I have a reservation.	**Tenho uma reserva.**
	teh • nyoo oo • muh reh • zehr • vuh
My name is…	**Chamo-me…**
	shuh • moo meh…
Do you have a room…?	**Tem um quarto…?**
	teng oong kwahr • too…
with a bathroom [toilet]/shower	**com quarto de banho/ chuveiro**
	kaum kwahr • too deh buh • nyoo/ shoo • vay • roo
with air conditioning	**com ar condicionado**
	kaum ar kawn • dee • seeoo • nah • thoo
that's smoking/ non-smoking	**para fumadores/ não-fumadores**
	puh • ruh foo • muh • daurz/nohm foo • muh • daurz
For…	**Para…**
	puh • ruh…
tonight	**hoje à noite**
	auzseh ah noyt
two nights	**duas noites**
	thoo • uhz noytz
one week	**uma semana**
	oo • muh seh • muh • nuh
Does the hotel have…?	**O hotel tem…?**
	oo aw • tehl teng…
a computer	**um computador**
	oong kaum • poo • tuh • daur

All types of accommodation can be found through the
Posto de Turismo (Tourist Information Center).

In Portugal **Turismo no Espaço Rural** offer privately owned
homes ranging from manor houses (**Turismo de Habitação**)
to country houses in rural settings (**Turismo Rural**) and
farmhouses (**Agro-tourism**).
In the Algarve and other seaside resorts, you should have
little trouble finding locals wanting to rent a room in their
own house.

Other accomodations options include:

Hotel
Hotels in Portugal are graded from 2-star to 5-star deluxe.
Hotel-Apartamento
Apartment hotels ranging from 2- to 4-star.
Hotel fazenda
Farmhouse lodges, generally equipped with a swimming
pool, tennis court and often horseback-riding facilities.
Pousada
A state-owned inn converted from an old castle, monastery,
convent, palace or in a location of interest to tourists.
Pensão
Corresponds to a boarding house. Usually divided into four
categories.
Pousada de juventude
Youth hostel; there are around 20 in Portugal.
Residencial
Bed and breakfast accommodations.

an elevator [lift]	**um elevador**
	oong eh • leh • <u>vuh</u> • daur
(wireless) internet service	**serviço de internet**
	sehr • <u>vee</u> • soo deh een • tehr • <u>neht</u>
room service	**serviço de quartos**
	sehr • <u>vee</u> • soo deh <u>kwahr</u> • tooz
a pool	**piscina**
	pee • <u>see</u> • nuh
a gym	**um ginásio**
	oong zsee • <u>nah</u> • zee • oo
I need...	**Preciso de...**
	preh • <u>see</u> • zoo deh...
an extra bed	**outra cama**
	<u>auoo</u> • truh <u>kuh</u> • muh
a cot	**cama de lona**
	<u>kuh</u> • muh deh <u>law</u> • nuh
a crib	**uma cama de bebé**
	<u>oo</u> • muh <u>kuh</u> • muh de beh • <u>beh</u>

For Numbers, see page 20.

PRICE

How much per night/ week?	**Quanto é por noite/semana?**
	<u>kwuhn</u> • too eh poor noyt/seh • <u>muh</u> • nuh
Are there any discounts?	**Há algum desconto?**
	ah ahl • goong dehs • kaum • too
Does the price include breakfast/ sales tax?	**O preço inclui o pequeno-almoço/ taxas?**
	oo <u>preh</u> • soo een • <u>kloo</u> • ee oo peh • <u>keh</u> • noo ahl • <u>mau</u> • soo/<u>tah</u> • shuhz
Are there any discounts?	**Há algum desconto?**
	ah ahl • goong dehs • kaum • too

YOU MAY HEAR...

O seu passaporte/cartão de crédito, por favor.
oo sehoo pah • suh • pawrt/kuhr • tohm deh kreh • dee • too poor fuh • vaur

Your passport/ credit card, please.

Preencha esta ficha, por favor.
pree • ehn shuh eh • stuh fee • shuh poor fuh • vaur

Please fill out this form.

Assine aqui.
uh • see • neh uh • kee

Sign here.

PREFERENCES

Can I see the room?	**Posso ver o quarto?**	
	paw • soo vehr oo kwahr • too	
I'd like a...room.	**Queria um... quarto.**	
	keh • ree • uh oong... kwahr • too	
better	**melhor**	
	meh • lyohr	
bigger	**maior**	
	muh • eeohr	
cheaper	**mais barato**	
	meyez buh • rah • too	
quieter	**mais silencioso**	
	meyez see • lehn • see • aw • zoo	
I'll take it.	**Fico com esse.**	
	fee • koo kaum eh • seh.	
No, I won't take it.	**Não, não fico com esse.**	
	nohm, nohm fee • koo kaum eh • seh	

QUESTIONS

Where's…?	**Onde é…?**
	aund eh…
the bar	**o bar**
	oo bar
the bathroom	**a casa de banho**
[toilet]	*uh kah • zuh deh buh • nyoo*
the elevator [lift]	**o elevador**
	oo eh • leh • vuh • daur
Can I have…?	**Pode arranjar-me…?**
	pawd uh • rrehn • zsahr • meh…
a blanket	**um cobertor**
	oong koo • behr • taur
an iron	**um ferro de engomar**
	oong feh • rroo deh ehn • goo • mahr
a pillow	**uma almofada**
	oo • muh ahl • moo • fah • duh
soap	**um sabonete**
	oong suh • boo • neht
toilet paper	**papel higiénico**
	puh • pehl ee • zseh • nee • koo
a towel	**uma toalha**
	oo • muh too • ah • lyuh
Do you have an adapter for this?	**Tem um adaptador para isto?**
	teng oong uh • duhp • tuh • daur puh • ruh ee • stoo
How do I turn on the lights?	**Como é que se acende as luzes?**
	kau • moo eh keh seh uh • sehn • deh uhz loo • zehz
Could you wake me at…?	**Podia acordar-me às…?**
	poo • dee • uh uh • koor • dahr • meh ahz…

Can I leave this in the safe?	**Posso deixar isto no cofre?** _paw_ • soo thay • _shahr ee_ • stoo noo _kaw_ • freh
I'd like to get my things from the safe.	**Queria tirar as minhas coisas do cofre.** keh • _ree_ • uh tee • _rahr_ uhz _mee_ • nyuhz _koy_ • zuhz thoo _kaw_ • freh
Is/Are there any mail/messages for me?	**Há correio/alguma mensagem para mim?** ah koo • _rray_ • oo/ahl • _goo_ • muh mehn • _sah_ • zseng _puh_ • ruh meeng
Do you have a laundry service?	**Tem serviço de lavandaria?** teng sehr • vee • soo deh luh • vuhn • deh • ree • uh

PROBLEMS

There's a problem.	**Há um problema.** ah oong proo • _bleh_ • muh
I've lost my key/ key card.	**Perdi a minha chave/carta de chave.** pehr • _dee_ uh _mee_ • nyuh shahv/_kahr_ • tuh deh shahv
I've locked myself out of my room.	**Fechei-me fora do quarto.** fee • _shay_ • meh _faw_ • ruh thoo _kwahr_ • too
There's no hot water/ toilet paper.	**Não há água quente/papel higiénico.** nohm ah _ah_ • gwuh kehnt/puh • _pehl_ ee • _zseh_ • nee • koo
The room is dirty.	**O quarto está sujo.** oo _kwahr_ • too ee • stah soo • _zsoo_
There are bugs in our room.	**Há insectos no quarto.** ah een • _sehk_ • tooz noo _kwahr_ • too
...doesn't work.	**...tem um defeito.** ...teng oong deh • _fay_ • too
Can you fix...?	**Pode arranjar...?** pawd uh • rrehn • _zsahr_...

the air conditioning	**o ar condicionado** *oo ar kawn • dee • seeoo • nah • thoo*
the fan	**a ventoinha** *uh vehn • too • ee • nyuh*
the heat [heating]	**o aquecimento** *oo uh • keh • see • mehn • too*
the lights	**as luzes** *uhz loo • zehz*
the TV	**a TV** *uh teh • veh*
the toilet	**a retrete** *uh reh • treht*
I'd like to move to another room.	**Queria mudar de quarto.** *keh • ree • uh moo • dahr deh kwahr • too*

Restrooms in Portugal are labeled W.C. Major cities have public toilets that are automatically sanitized after each use. They are found on the street and have a small fee per use. Some of these public restrooms have 20-minute time limits, and the door will automatically open when your time is up.

In hotels and private residences, it is standard for bathrooms to be equipped with bidets.

YOU MAY SEE...

EMPURRAR/PUXAR	push/pull
CASA DE BANHO/	bathroom/
LAVABOS	restroom [toilet]
CHUVEIRO	shower
ELEVADOR	elevator [lift]
ESCADAS	stairs
LAVANDARIA	laundry
NÃO PERTURBAR	do not disturb
PORTA DE INCÊNDIO	fire door
SAÍDA (DE EMERGÊNCIA)	(emergency) exit
CHAMADA PARA DESPERTAR	wake-up call

CHECKING OUT

When's check-out?	**A que horas temos de deixar o quarto?**
	uh kee aw • ruhz teh • mooz deh
	thay • shahr oo kwahr • too
Could I leave my bags here until...?	**Posso deixar a minha bagagem aqui até...?**
	paw • soo day • shahr uh mee • nyuh
	buh • gah • zseng uh • kee uh • teh...
Can I have an itemized bill/ a receipt?	**Pode dar-me uma conta detalhada/uma factura?**
	pawd dahr • meh oo • muh kaum • tuh
	deh • tuh • lyah • duh/oo • muh
	fah • too • ruh
I think there's a mistake.	**Creio que se enganou.**
	kray • oo keh seh ehn • guh • nau

I'll pay in cash/by credit card.

Pago com dinheiro/com o cartão de crédito.

pah • _goo kaum dee_ • _nyay_ • _roo/kaum oo kuhr_ • _tohm deh kreh_ • _dee_ • _too_

The 220-volt, 50-cycle AC is the norm throughout Portugal. Note that if you bring your own electrical appliances, you will need to buy an adapter plug (for round pins, not square) before leaving home as it will be difficult to purchase one whilst in Portugal.

A service charge is generally added to your hotel and restaurant bills. However, if the service has been particularly good, you may want to leave an extra tip. The following chart is a guide:

Bellman, per bag	€1
Hotel maid, per day	€1
Restroom attendant	€0.20

RENTING

I reserved an apartment/a room.

Reservei um apartamento/quarto.

reh • _zehr_ • _vay_ oong uh • _puhr_ • _tuh_ • _mehn_ • _too/ kwahr_ • _too_

My name is…

Chamo-me…

shuh • _moo meh…_

Can I have the key/key card?	**Posso ter a chave/carta de chave?**
	paw • soo tehr uh shahv/kahr • tuh deh shahv
Are there...?	**Há...?**
	_ah..._
dishes	**a louça**
	uh lau • suh
pillows	**almofadas**
	ahl • moo • fah • duhz
sheets	**lençóis**
	lehn • soyz
towels	**toalhas**
	too • ah • lyuhz
utensils [cutlery]	**os talheres**
	ooz tuh • lyeh • rehz
When do I put out the the bins/recycling?	**Quando ponho o lixo/o lixo para reciclar lá fora?**
	kwuhn • doo paw • nyoo oo lee • shoo/lee • shoo puh • ruh ree • see • klahr lah faw • ruh
...is broken.	**...está partido m/partida f.**
	...ee • stah puhr • tee • thoo/puhr • tee • thuh
How does...work?	**Como funciona...?**
	kau • moo faun • see • aw • nuh...
the air conditioner	**o ar condicionado**
	oo ar kawn • dee • seeoo • nah • thoo
the dishwasher	**a máquina de lavar pratos**
	uh mah • kee • nuh deh luh • vahr prah • tooz
the freezer	**a arca frigorífica**
	uh ahr • kuh free • goo • ree • fee • kuh
the heater	**o aquecedor**
	oo uh • keh • seh • daur

the microwave	**o microondas**
	oo mee • krau • aun • duhz
the refrigerator	**o frigorífico**
	oo free • goo • ree • fee • koo
the stove	**o fogão**
	oo foo • gohm
the washing machine	**a máquina de lavar (roupa)**
	uh mah • kee • nuh deh luh • vahr (rauoo • puh)

DOMESTIC ITEMS

I need…	**Preciso de…**
	preh • see • zoo deh…
an adapter	**um adaptador**
	oong uh • duhp • tuh • daur
aluminum [kitchen] foil	**papel de alumínio**
	puh • pehl deh uh • loo • mee • nee • oo
a bottle opener	**um abre-garrafas**
	oong ah • breh • guh • rrah • fuhz
a broom	**uma vassoura**
	oo • muh vuh • sau • ruh
a can opener	**um abre-latas**
	oong ah • breh • lah • tuhz
cleaning supplies	**produtos de limpeza**
	prau • thoo • tooz deh leem • peh • zuh
a corkscrew	**um saca-rolhas**
	oong sah • kuh • rau • lyuz
I need…	**Preciso de…**
	preh • see • zoo deh…
detergent	**detergente em pó para a roupa**
	deh • tehr • zsehnt eng paw puh • ruh uh rauoo • puh
dishwashing liquid	**detergente para a louça**
	deh • tehr • zsehnt puh • ruh uh lau • suh

bin bags	**sacos para o lixo**
	sah • kooz _puh_ • ruh oo _lee_ • shoo
a light bulb	**uma lâmpada eléctrica**
	_oo_ • muh _luhm_ • puh • duh ee • _leh_ • tree • kuh
matches	**fósforos**
	fawz • fuh • rooz
a mop	**o esfregão**
	oo ees • fruh • _gohm_
paper napkins	**guardanapos de papel**
	gwahr • duh • _nah_ • pooz deh puh • _pehl_
paper towels	**papel da cozinha**
	puh • _pehl_ duh koo • _zee_ • nyuh
plastic wrap [cling film]	**papel aderente**
	puh • _pehl_ uh • deh • _rehnt_
a plunger	**um desentupidor**
	oong deh • _zehn_ • too • pee • _daur_
scissors	**uma tesoura**
	_oo_ • muh teh • _zau_ • ruh
a vacuum cleaner	**um aspirador**
	oong uh • spee • ruh • _daur_

For In the Kitchen, see page 192.

AT THE HOSTEL

Do you have any places left for tonight?	**Ainda há vagas para hoje à noite?**
	uh • _een_ • duh ah _vah_ • guhz _puh_ • ruh auzseh _ah_ noyt
Can I have…?	**Pode dar-me…?**
	pawd _dahr_ • meh…
a single/double room	**um quarto individual/duplo**
	oong _kwahr_ • too een • dee • vee • doo • _ahl_/ _doo_ • ploo

There are only around twenty youth hostels in Portugal. In Portugal, prices for a room at a hostel range anywhere from seventeen to sixty-five euros and are good value for money.

In order to stay in a hostel in Portugal, you must be under the age of twenty-six and have a Youth Card. If you do not have a Youth Card, you can purchase one at the hostel upon your arrival. The Youth Card is only valid until your twenty-sixth birthday.

a blanket	**um cobertor**
	oong koo • behr • taur
a pillow	**uma almofada**
	oo • muh ahl • moo • fah • duh
sheets	**lençóis**
	lehn • soyz
a towel	**uma toalha**
	oo • muh too • ah • lyuh
Do you have lockers?	**Tem cacifos?**
	teng kuh • see • fooz
What time are the doors locked?	**A que horas fecham as portas?**
	uh keh aw • ruhz feh • shohm uhz pawr • tuhz
Do I need a membership card?	**Preciso de cartão de sócio?**
	preh • see • zoo deh kuhr • tohm deh saw • see • oo
Here's my international student card.	**Aqui está o meu cartão internacional de estudante.**
	uh • kee ee • stah oo mehoo kuhr • tohm een • tehr • nuh • seeoo • nahl de ee • stoo • duhnt

GOING CAMPING

Can I camp here?	**Posso acampar aqui?**
	paw • soo uh • kuhm • pahr uh • kee
Where's the campsite?	**Onde é o parque de campismo [camping]?**
	aund eh oo pahr • keh deh kuhm • peez • moo [kuhm • peeng]
What is the charge per day/week?	**Qual é a tarifa por dia/semana?**
	kwahl eh uh tuh • ree • fuh poor dee • uh/ seh • muh • nuh
Are there…?	**Há…?** *ah…*
cooking facilities	**uma área para se cozinhar**
	oo • muh ah • ree • uh puh • ruh seh koo • zee • nyahr
electrical outlets	**electricidade**
	ee • leh • tree • see • dahd
laundry facilities	**uma lavandaria**
	oo • muh luh • vuhn • deh • ree • uh
Are there…?	**Há…?**
	ah…
showers	**o chuveiro**
	oo shoo • vay • roo
tents for rent [hire]	**tendas para aluguer**
	tehn • duhz puh • ruh uh • loo • gehr
Where can I empty the chemical toilet?	**Onde posso esvaziar o banheiro químico?**
	aund paw • soo ees • vee • ahr oo buh • nyay • roo kee • mee • koo

YOU MAY SEE...

ÁGUA POTÁVEL	drinking water
É PROIBIDO ACAMPAR	no camping
É PROIBIDO ACENDER FOGOS/	no fires/
CHURRASCAR	barbecues

COMMUNICATIONS

NEED TO KNOW

Where's an internet café?	**Onde fica um internet café?** *aund fee • kuh oong een • tehr • neht kuh • feh*
Can I access the Internet here?	**Tenho acesso à internet aqui?** *teh • nyoo uh • seh • soo ah een • tehr • neht uh • kee*
Can I check e-mail here?	**Posso ler o meu e-mail aqui?** *paw • soo lehr oo mehoo ee • mehl uh • khee*
How much per (half) hour?	**Quanto é por (meia) hora?** *kwuhn • too eh poor (may • uh) aw • ruh*
How do I connect/ log on?	**Como conecto/faço o logon?** *kau • moo koo • nehk • too/fah • soo oo law • gawn*
A phone card, please.	**Um credifone, se faz favor.** *oong kreh • dee • faun seh fahz fuh • vaur*

Can I have your phone number?	**Pode dar-me o seu número de telefone?**
	pawd dahr • meh oo sehoo noo • meh • roo deh tehl • fawn
Here's my number/ e-mail address.	**Este é o meu número/e-mail.**
	ehst eh oo mehoo noo • meh • roo/ ee • mehl
Call me.	**Telefone-me.**
	tehl • fawn • eh • meh
E-mail me.	**Envie-me um e-mail.**
	ehn • vee • eh meh oong ee • mehl
Hello. This is…	**Estou…**
	ee • stawoo
I'd like to speak to…	**Queria falar com…**
	keh • ree • uh fuh • lahr kaum…
Could you repeat that, please?	**Importa-se de repetir, por favor?**
	eem • pawr • tuh • seh deh reh • peh • teer poor fuh • vaur
I'll call back later.	**Chamo mais tarde.**
	shuh • moo meyez tahr • deh
Bye.	**Adeus.**
	uh • deeoosh
Where's the post office?	**Onde são os correios?**
	aund sohm ooz koo • rray • ooz
I'd like to send this to…	**Gostaria de mandar isto para…**
	goo • stuh • ree • uh deh muhn • dahr ee • stoo puh • ruh…

ONLINE

Where's an internet cafe?	**Onde fica um internet café?**
	aund fee • kuh oong een • tehr • neht kuh • feh
Does it have wireless internet?	**Tem internet wireless?**
	teng een • tehr • neht wire • less
What is the WiFi password?	**Qual é a senha do WiFi?**
	kwahl eh uh seh • nyuh doo WiFi
Is the WiFi free?	**O WiFi é grátis?**
	oo WiFi eh grah teez
Do you have bluetooth?	**Tem bluetooth?**
	teng bluetooth
How do I turn the computer on/off?	**Como ligo/desligo o computador?**
	kau • moo lee • goo/dehz • lee • goo oo kaum • poo • tuh • daur
Can I...?	**Posso...?**
	paw • soo...
access the internet	**aceder a internet**
	uh • seh • dehr uh een • tehr • neht
check e-mail	**ler o meu e-mail**
	lehr oo mehoo ee • mehl
print	**imprimir**
	eeng • pree • meer
How much per (half) hour?	**Quanto é por (meia) hora?**
	kwuhn • too eh poor (may • uh) aw • ruh
How do I...?	**Como...?**
	kau • moo...
connect/ disconnect	**conecto/desconecto**
	koo • nehk • too/dehz • koo • nehk • too
log on/off	**faço o logon/logoff**
	fah • soo oo law • gawn/law • gawf
type this symbol	**bato este símbolo**
	bah • too ehst seem • boo • loo

What's your e-mail? **Qual é o seu e-mail?**
kwahl eh oo sehoo ee • mehl

My e-mail is… **O meu e-mail é…**
oo mehoo ee • mehl eh…

Do you have a **Tem um scanner?**
scanner? *teng oong scanner*

YOU MAY SEE...

FECHAR	close
APAGAR	delete
E-MAIL	e-mail
SAÍDA	exit
AJUDA	help
MESSENGER	instant messenger
INTERNET	internet
LOGIN	login
(NOVA) MENSAGEM	(new) message
LIGADO/DESLIGADO	on/off
ABRIR	open
IMPRIMIR [IMPRESSAR]	print
GUARDAR	save
ENVIAR	send
NOME DO UTILIZADOR [USUÁRIO]/	username/
SENHA	password
INTERNET WIRELESS	wireless internet

SOCIAL MEDIA

Are you on **Está no Facebook/Twitter?**
Facebook/Twitter? *ee • stah noo Facebook/Twitter*

What's your user name?	**Qual é o seu nome de utilizador?**
	kwahl eh oo sehoo naum • eh deh oo • tee • lee • zuh • daur
I'll add you as a friend.	**Vou adicioná-lo como amigo.**
	vawoo • oo uh • dee • seeoo • nah • loo kau • moo uh • mee • goo
I'll follow you on Twitter.	**Vou segui-lo no Twitter.**
	vawoo • oo seh • gee • loo noo Twitter
Are you following...?	**Está a seguir...?**
	ee • stah uh seh • geer...
I'll put the pictures on Facebook/Twitter.	**Vou colocar as fotos no Facebook/Twitter.**
	vawoo koo • loo • khahr uhz faw • tawz noo Facebook/Twitter
I'll tag you in the pictures.	**Vou identificá-lo nas fotos.**
	vawoo ee • dehnt • tee • fee • kah • loo nuhz faw • tawz.

PHONE

A phone card/ prepaid phone, please.	**Um credifone/cartão de telefone pré-pago, por favor.**
	oong kreh • dee • fawn/kuhr • tohm deh tehl • fawn preh • pah • goo poor fuh • vaur
How much?	**Quanto é?**
	kwuhn • too eh
Where's the pay phone?	**Onde está o telefone pago?**
	aund ee • stah oo tehl • fawn pah • goo
My phone doesn't work here.	**O meu telefone não funciona aqui.**
	oo meehoo tehl • fawn nohm foon • seeaw • nuh uh • kee
What network are you on?	**Em que rede está?**
	eng keh rreh • deh ee • stah
Is it 3G?	**É 3G?**
	eh trehz zseh

I have run out of credit/minutes.	**Fiquei sem crédito/minutos.** *fee • kay seng kreh • dee • too/ mee • noo • tooz*
Can I buy some credit?	**Posso comprar algum crédito?** *paw • soo kaum • prahr ahl • goong kreh • dee • too?*
Do you have a phone charger?	**Tem um carregador de telefone?** *teng oong kah • rreh • guh • daur deh tehl • fawn*
What's the area/country code for…?	**Qual é o código de área/país para…?** *kwahl eh oo <u>kaw</u> • dee • goo deh ah • <u>eh</u> • ree • uh/puh <u>eez puh</u> • ruh…*
What's the number for Information?	**Qual é o número das Informações?** *kwahl eh oo <u>noo</u> • meh • roo duhz eeng • foor • muh • <u>soingz</u>*
I'd like the number for…	**Queria o número para…** *keh • <u>ree</u> • uh oo <u>noo</u> • meh • roo <u>puh</u> • ruh…*
I'd like to call collect [reverse the charges].	**Queria telefonar a cobrar no destino.** *keh • ree • uh tehl • fawn • ahr uh koo • brahr noo dehz • tee • noo*
Can I have your number?	**Pode dar-me o seu número de telefone?** *pawd <u>dahr</u> • meh oo sehoo <u>noo</u> • meh • roo deh tehl • <u>fawn</u>*
Here's my number.	**Este é o meu número.** *ehst eh oo mehoo <u>noo</u> • meh • roo*
Call me.	**Telefone-me.** *tehl • <u>faw</u> • neh • meh*
Text me.	**Manda-me uma mensagem de texto.** *<u>muhn</u> • duh • meh <u>oo</u> • muh mehn • <u>sah</u> • zseng deh <u>tehk</u> • stoo*
I'll call you.	**Eu ligo.** *eeoo <u>lee</u> • guh*
I'll text you.	**Mando-te uma mensagem de texto.** *<u>muhn</u> • doo • teh <u>oo</u> • muh mehn • <u>sah</u> • zseng deh <u>tehk</u> • stoo*

TELEPHONE ETIQUETTE

Hello. This is…	**Estou … Fala…**
	_ee_ • stoo. _fah_ • luh…
I'd like to speak to…	**Queria falar com…**
	keh • _ree_ • uh fuh • _lahr_ kaum…
Extension…	**Extensão…**
	ehs • tehn • _sohm_…
Speak louder/more slowly, please.	**Fale mais alto/devagar, por favor.**
	fah • leh meyez _ahl_ • too/deh • vuh • _gahr_ poor fuh • _vaur_
Could you repeat that?	**Importa-se de repetir?**
	eeng • _pawr_ • tuh • seh deh reh • peh • _teer_
I'll call back later.	**Eu ligo mais tarde.**
	eeoo _lee_ • _guh_ meyez tahrd
Bye.	**Adeus.**
	uh • _deeooz_

For Numbers, see page 20.

There are over fifty thousand pay phones located throughout Portugal, operated by **PT Comunicações**. They are easy to use and offer different payment options with coins, phone cards, credit cards and ATM cards. Temporary mobile phones with 'pay as you go' plans are also available and may be more convenient. Internet cafes are increasingly popular to check e-mail and surf the net, and some public places do offer wireless internet access so that you can connect from your laptop.

YOU MAY HEAR...

Quem fala?
keng fah • luh

Who's calling?

Não desligue.
nohm dehs • lee • geh

Hold on.

Vou-o ligar agora.
vauoo • oo lee • gahr uh • gaw • ruh

I'll put you through.

Lamento, mas ele/ela não está.
luh • mehn • too muhz ehl/ehl • uh nohm ee • stah

I'm afraid he's/she's not in.

Ele/Ela não pode atender o telefone.
ehl/ehl • uh nohm pawd uh • tehn • dehr oo tehl • fawn

He/She can't come to the phone.

Quer deixar uma mensagem?
kehr day • shahr oo • muh mehn • sah • zseng

Would you like to leave a message?

Ligue mais tarde/daqui dez minutos.
lee • geh meyez tahr • deh/da • kee • uh dehz mee • noo • tooz

Call back later/in ten minutes.

Ele/Ela pode telefonar-lhe?
ehl/ehl • uh pawd tehl • fawn • ahr ly

Can he/she call you back?

Qual é o seu número de telefone?
kwahl eh oo sehoo noo • meh • roo deh tehl • fawn

What's your number?

FAX

Can I send/receive a fax here?

Posso enviar/receber um fax aqui?
paw • soo ehn • vee • ahr/reh • seh • behr oong fahks uh • kee

What's the fax number?

Qual é o número de fax?
kwahl eh oo noo • meh • roo deh fahks

| Please fax this to… | **Por favor mande este fax para…** |
| | *poor fuh • <u>vaur</u> <u>muhn</u> • deh ehst fahks <u>puh</u> • ruh…* |

POST

Where's the post office/mailbox [postbox]?	**Onde é que é o correio/a caixa do correio?**
	aund eh keh eh oo koo • <u>rray</u> • oo/uh <u>keye</u> • shuh thoo koo • <u>rray</u> • oo
A stamp for this postcard/letter, please.	**Um selo para este postal/esta carta, se faz favor.**
	oong <u>seh</u> • loo <u>puh</u> • ruh ehst poo • <u>stahl/</u> <u>eh</u> • stuh <u>kahr</u> • tuh seh fahz fuh • <u>vaur</u>
How much?	**Quanto é?**
	<u>kwuhn</u> • too eh
I want to send this package by airmail/ express.	**Queria mandar este embrulho por via aérea/correio expresso.**
	keh • <u>ree</u> • uh muhn • <u>dahr</u> <u>eh</u> • stuh ehm • <u>broo</u> • lyoo poor <u>vee</u> • uh uh • <u>eh</u> • ree • uh/koo • <u>rray</u> • oo ees • <u>preh</u> • soo
A receipt, please.	**Um recibo, se faz favor.**
	oong reh • <u>see</u> • boo seh fahz fuh • <u>vaur</u>

Post offices in Portugal are indicated by signs reading
CTT (**Correios e Telecomunicações**). Hours are
generally Monday to Friday from 9:00 a.m. to 6:00 p.m.; the
main (larger) offices are also open on Saturday and Sunday
from 9:00 a.m. to 5:00 p.m.
Note that red mailboxes are for **correio normal** (normal
mail) and blue mailboxes are for **correio azul** (express mail).
For international mail, use the blue express box unless
otherwise indicated.
Stamps can be bought at post offices or at any shop bearing
the sign of the red horse symbol.

YOU MAY HEAR...

Por favor preencha a declaração da alfândega.
*poor fuh • vaur pree • ehn • shuh uh
deh • kluh • ruh • sohm duh
uhl • fuhn • dee • guh*

Please fill out the customs declaration form.

Qual é o valor?
kwahl eh oo vuh • laur

What's the value?

O que é que tem dentro?
oo kee eh keh teng dehn • troo

What's inside?

SIGHTSEEING

NEED TO KNOW

Where's the tourist office?	**Onde é o posto de turismo?** *aund eh oo pau•stoo deh too•reez•moo*
What are the main points of interest?	**O que há de mais interessante para se ver?** *oo kee ah deh meyez een•tehr•reh•suhnt puh•ruh seh vehr*
Do you have tours in English?	**Tem excursões em inglês?** *teng ee•skoor•soings eng eng•lehz*
Can I have a map/ guide?	**Pode dar-me um mapa/guia?** *pawd dahr•meh oong mah•puh/ gee•uh*

TOURIST INFORMATION

Do you have any information on...?	**Tem informação sobre...?** *teng een•foor•muh•sohm sau•breh...*
Can you recommend...?	**Pode recomendar-me...?** *pawd reh•koo•mehn•dahr•meh...*
a boat trip	**uma excursão de barco** *oo•muh ee•skoor•sohm deh bahr•koo*
an excursion	**uma excursão** *oo•muh ee•skoor•sohm*
a sightseeing tour	**um circuito turístico** *oong seer•koo•ee•too too•ree•stee•koo*

i

In Portugal, town maps and brochures on main tourist attractions are available at airports and from tourist information centers. Ask at your hotel or check online to find the nearest office.

ON TOUR

I'd like to go on the tour to…	**Gostaria de ir na excursão para…** *goo • stuh • ree • uh deh eer nuh ee • skoor • sohm puh • ruh…*
When's the next tour?	**Quando é a próxima excursão?** *kwuhn • doo eh uh praw • see • muh ee • skoor • sohm*
Are there tours in English?	**Há excursões em inglês?** *ah ee • skoor • soings eng eeng • lehz*
Is there an English-speaking guide/audio guide?	**Há algum guia que fale inglês/uma gravação da visita guiada em inglês?** *ah ahl • goong gee • uh keh fah • leh eeng • lehz/oo • muh gruh • vuh • sohm deh vee • zee • tuh gee • ah • duh eng eeng • lehz*
What time do we leave/return?	**Quando saímos/regressemos?** *kwuhn • doo suh • eemooz/ reh • greh • seh • mooz*
We'd like to see…	**Gostaríamos de ver…** *goo • stuh • ree • uh • mooz deh vehr…*
Can we stop here…?	**Podemos parar aqui…?** *poo • deh • mooz puh • rahr uh • kee…*
to take photographs	**para tirar fotografias** *puh • ruh tee • rahr foo • too • gruh • fee • uhz*

to buy souvenirs	**para comprar lembranças**	
	puh • ruh kaum • prahr leng • bruhn • suhz	
to use the restrooms [toilets]	**para usar as casas de banho**	
	puh • ruh oo • zahr uhz kah • zuhz deh buh • nyoo	
Is there access for the disabled?	**Há algum acesso para os deficientes?**	
	ah ahl • goong uh • seh • soo puh • ruh ooz deh • fee • see • ehntz	

For Disabled Travelers, see page 160.

SEEING THE SIGHTS

Where is/are…?	**Onde é/são…?**	
	aund eh/sohm…	
the battleground	**o campo de batalha**	
	oo kuhm • poo deh buh • tah • lyuh	
the botanical garden	**o jardim botânico**	
	oo zsuhr • deeng boo • tuh • nee • koo	
the castle	**o castelo**	
	oo kuhz • teh • loo	
the downtown area	**o centro da cidade**	
	oo sehn • troo duh see • dahd	
the fountain	**a fonte**	
	uh faun • teh	
the library	**a biblioteca**	
	uh bee • blee • aw • teh • kuh	
the market	**o mercado**	
	oo mehr • kah • doo	
the museum	**o museu**	
	oo moo • zehoo	
the old town	**a parte velha da cidade**	
	uh pahrt veh • lyuh duh see • dahd	
the palace	**o palácio**	
	oo puh • lah • see • yoo	

the park	**o parque**
	oo pahr • keh
the ruins	**as ruínas**
	uhz roo • een • uhz
the shopping area	**a zona comercial**
	uh zau • nuh koo • mehr • see • ahl
the town square	**a praça central**
	uh prah • suh sehn • trahl
Can you show me on the map?	**Pode indicar-me no mapa?**
	pawd een • dee • kahr • meh noo mah • puh
It's…	**É…**
	eh…
amazing	**espantoso**
	ee • spuhn • tau • zoo
beautiful	**lindo**
	leen • doo
boring	**aborrecido**
	uh • boo • rreh • see • thoo
interesting	**interessante**
	een • teh • reh • suhnt
magnificent	**magnífico**
	mahg • nee • fee • koo
romantic	**romântico**
	roo • muhn • tee • koo
strange	**estranho**
	ee • struh • nyoo
stunning	**estupendo**
	ee • stoo • pehn • doo
terrible	**horrível**
	aw • rree • vehl
ugly	**feio**
	fay • oo
I (don't) like any of it.	**(Não) gosto de tudo.**
	(nohm) gaw • stoo deh too • thoo

RELIGIOUS SITES

Where's…?	**Onde é…?**
	aund eh…
the cathedral	**a catedral**
	uh keh • teh • drahl
the Catholic/	**a igreja católica/protestante**
Protestant church	*uh ee • gray • zsuh kuh • taw • lee • kuh/*
	praw • tee • stuhnt
the mosque	**a mesquita**
	uh mehz • kee • tuh
Where's…?	**Onde é…?**
	aund eh…
the shrine	**o relicário**
	oo reh • lee • kah • ree • oo
the synagogue	**a sinagoga**
	uh seen • uh • gaw • guh
the temple	**o templo**
	oo tehm • ploo
What time is mass/	**A que horas é a missa/o culto?**
the service?	*uh kee aw • ruhz eh uh mee • suh/oo*
	kool • too

For Asking Directions, see page 66.

LEISURE TIME

SHOPPING 104

SPORT & LEISURE 126

TRAVELING WITH CHILDREN 136

SHOPPING

NEED TO KNOW

Where is the market/ mall [shopping center]?	**Onde é o mercado/o centro comercial?**
	aund eh oo mehr • <u>kah</u> • thoo/oo <u>sehn</u> • troo koo • mehr • see • ahl
I'm just looking.	**Estou só a ver.**
	ee • <u>stawoo</u> saw uh vehr
Can you help me?	**Pode ajudar-me?**
	pawd uh • zsoo • <u>dahr</u> • meh
I'm being helped.	**Alguém está a ajudar-me.**
	ahl • <u>gehng</u> ee • <u>stah</u> uh uh • zsoo • <u>dahr</u> • meh
How much is it?	**Quanto é?**
	kwuhn • too eh
That one, please.	**Aquele** *m/***Aquela** *f***, por favor.**
	uh • <u>kehl</u>/uh • <u>keh</u> • luh poor fuh • <u>vaur</u>
That's all, thanks.	**É tudo, obrigado** *m/***obrigada** *f.*
	eh <u>too</u> • doo aw • bree • <u>gah</u> • doo/ aw • bree • <u>gah</u> • thuh
Where can I pay?	**Onde pago?**
	aund <u>pah</u> • goo
I'll pay in cash/ by credit card.	**Pago com dinheiro/com o cartão de crédito.**
	<u>pah</u> • goo kaum dee • <u>nyay</u> • roo/kaum oo kuhr • <u>tohm</u> deh <u>kreh</u> • dee • too
A receipt, please.	**Um recibo, se faz favor.**
	oong reh • <u>see</u> • boo seh fahz fuh • <u>vaur</u>

Flea markets in Portugal are common in almost every town and usually occur once a week or every other week (in smaller towns). These are the best places to get the most for your money. Haggling is common and almost expected. It is rare to pay full price for anything except food, for which prices are generally not negotiable. Bring cash, as few vendors accept credit cards.

AT THE SHOPS

Where is/are...?	**Onde é/são...?** *aund eh/sohm...*
the antiques store	**a loja das antiguidades** *uh <u>law</u> • zsuh duhz* *uhn • tee • gee • <u>dah</u> • dehz*
the bakery	**a padaria** *uh pah • deh • <u>ree</u> • uh*
the bank	**o banco** *oo <u>buhn</u> • koo*
the bookstore	**a livraria** *uh lee • vreh • <u>ree</u> • uh*
the clothing store	**a loja de artigos de vestuário** *uh <u>law</u> • zsuh deh uhr • <u>tee</u> • gooz de* *veh • stoo • <u>ah</u> • ree • oo*
the delicatessen	**a charcutaria** *uh shuhr • koo • tuh • <u>ree</u> • uh*
the department store	**o grande armazém** *oo gruhnd uhr • muh • <u>zeng</u>*
the gift shop	**a loja de recordações** *uh <u>law</u> • zsuh deh reh • kaur • duh • <u>soingz</u>*

the health food store	**a loja de produtos dietéticos** *uh law•zsuh deh proo•doo•tooz dee•eh•tee•kooz*
the jeweler	**a joalharia** *uh zsoo•uh•lyuh•ree•uh*
the liquor store [off-licence]	**a loja de vinhos** *uh law•zsuh deh vee•nyooz*
the market	**o mercado** *oo mehr•kah•doo*
the music store	**a loja de música** *uh law•zsuh deh moo•zee•cuh*
Where is/are...?	**Onde é/são...?** *aund eh/sohm...*
the pastry shop	**a pastelaria** *uh puh•stuh•luh•ree•uh*
the pharmacy [chemist]	**a farmácia** *uh fuhr•mah•see•uh*
the produce [grocery] store	**a frutaria** *uh froo•tuh•ree•uh*
the shoe store	**a sapataria** *uh suh•puh•tuh•ree•uh*
the shopping mall [shopping centre]	**o centro comercial** *oo sehn•troo koo•mehr•see•ahl*
the souvenir store	**a loja de lembranças** *uh law•zsuh deh lehn•bruhn•suhz*
the supermarket	**o supermercado** *oo soo•pehr•mehr•kah•thoo*
the tobacconist	**a tabacaria** *uh tuh•bah•kuh•ree•uh*
the toy store	**o armazém de brinquedos** *oo ahr•muh•zehn deh breeng•keh•dooz*

ASK AN ASSISTANT

What are the opening hours?	**Qual a hora de abertura?** *kwahl uh <u>aw</u> • ruh deh ah • behr • <u>too</u> • ruh*
Where is/are...?	**Onde é/são...?** *aund eh/sohm...*
the cashier	**a caixa** *uh <u>keye</u> • shuh*
the escalator	**a escada rolante** *uh ees • <u>kah</u> • duh roo • <u>luhnt</u>*
the elevator [lift]	**o elevador** *oo eh • leh • vuh • <u>daur</u>*
the fitting room	**os vestiários** *ooz vehs • tee • <u>ah</u> • ree • ooz*
the store directory [guide]	**a planta da loja** *uh <u>pluhn</u> • tuh duh <u>law</u> • zsuh*
Can you help me?	**Pode ajudar-me?** *pawd uh • zsoo • <u>dahr</u> • meh*
I'm just looking.	**Estou só a ver.** *ee • <u>stawoo</u> saw uh vehr*
I'm being helped.	**Alguém está a ajudar-me.** *ahl • <u>geng</u> ee • <u>stah</u> uh uh • zsoo • <u>dahr</u> • meh*

Do you have…?	**Tem…?**
	teng…
Could you show me…?	**Podia mostrar-me…?**
	poo • dee • uh mooz • trahr • meh…
Can you ship it/ wrap it ?	**Pode despachá-lo/embrulhá-lo?**
	pawd dehs • puh • shah • loo/ eng • broo • lyah • loo
How much is it?	**Quanto é?**
	kwuhn • too eh
That's all, thanks.	**É tudo, obrigado** *m*/**obrigada** *f.*
	eh too • doo aw • bree • gah • doo/ aw • bree • gah • duh

YOU MAY HEAR…

Deseja alguma coisa?
deh • zay • zuh ahl • goo • muh koy • zuh
Would you like something?

Um momento.
oong moo • mehn • too
One moment.

O que é que deseja?
oo kee eh keh deh • zay • zsuh
What would you like?

Mais alguma coisa?
meyez ahl • goo • muh koy • zuh
Anything else?

YOU MAY SEE…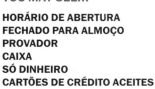

HORÁRIO DE ABERTURA	opening hours
FECHADO PARA ALMOÇO	closed for lunch
PROVADOR	fitting room
CAIXA	cashier
SÓ DINHEIRO	cash only
CARTÕES DE CRÉDITO ACEITES	credit cards accepted

PERSONAL PREFERENCES

I'd like something…	**Queria uma coisa…**
	keh • ree • uh oo • muh koy • zuh…
cheap/expensive	**barata/cara**
	buh • rah • tuh/kah • ruh
larger/smaller	**maior/mais pequena**
	meye • awr/meyez peh • keh • nuh
from this region	**desta região**
	dehs • tuh ree • zsee • ohm
Around… euros.	**Cerca de… euros.**
	sehr • ka deh… ehoo • rooz
Is it real?	**É verdadeiro?**
	eh vehr • duh • day • roo
Could you show me this/that?	**Podia mostrar-me este/esse?**
	poo • dee • uh moos • trahr • meh ehst/ehs
That's not quite what I want.	**Não é bem o que quero.**
	nohm eh beng oo keh keh • roo
No, I don't like it.	**Não, não gosto.**
	nohm nohm gaw • stoo
It's too expensive.	**É caro demais.**
	eh kah • roo deh • meyez
I have to think about it.	**Tenho que pensar nisto.**
	tay • nyoo keh pehn • sahr nee • stoo
I'll take it.	**Levo.**
	leh • voo

For Clothing, see page 116.

PAYING & BARGAINING

How much?	**Quanto é?**
	kwuhn • too eh
I'll pay…	**Pago…**
	pah • goo…

in cash	**com dinheiro**
	kaum dee • nyay • roo
by credit card	**com o cartão de crédito**
	kaum oo kuhr • tohm deh kreh • dee • too
by traveler's check [cheque]	**com livro de cheques**
	kaum lee • vroo deh sheh • kehz
A receipt, please.	**Um recibo, se faz favor.**
	oong reh • see • boo seh fahz fuh • vaur
That's too much.	**Isso é muito.**
	ee • soo eh mooee • too
I'll give you…	**Vou dar-lhe…**
	vau dahr • lyeh…
I only have…euros/ reais.	**Só tenho…euros/reais.**
	saw teh • nyoo… eeoo • rooz/rree • eyez
Is that your best price?	**É o preço melhor que me pode dar?**
	eh oo preh • soo mee • lyawr keh meh pawd dahr
Can you give me a discount?	**Pode-me dar um desconto?**
	pawd • meh dahr oong dehs • kaun • too

For Numbers, see page 20.

The most commonly used bank cards are Visa™, American Express®, Europay/Mastercard™, JCB and Maestro®. In some small villages and towns and at markets, cash may still be the only form of currency accepted.

YOU MAY HEAR...

Como deseja pagar?
kau • moo deh • zay • zsuh puh • gahr

How are you paying?

Esta transacção não foi autorizada.
eh • stuh truhn • suh • sohm nohm foy ahoo • too • ree • zah • thuh

This transaction was not authorized.

Não aceitamos cartões de crédito.
nohm uh • say • tuh • mooz kuhr • toings deh kreh • dee • too

We don't accept credit cards.

Só com dinheiro, por favor.
saw kaum dee • nyay • roo poor fuh • vaur

Cash only, please.

Não tem troco?
nohm teng trau • koo

Do you have any smaller bills?

A identificação, por favor.
uh ee • dehnt • tee • fee • kuh • sohm, poor fuh • vaur

ID, please.

MAKING A COMPLAINT

I'd like...	**Queria...**
	keh • ree • uh...
to exchange this	**trocar isto**
	troo • kahr ee • stoo
to return this	**retornar isto**
	ree • tawrr • nahr ee • stoo
a refund	**um reembolso**
	oong ree • eng • baul • soo
to see the manager	**falar com o gerente** _m_/**a gerente** _f_
	fuh • lahr kaum oo zseh • rehnt/uh zseh • rehnt

SERVICES

Can you recommend…?	**Pode recomendar-me…?** *pawd reh • koo • mehn • <u>dahr</u> • meh…*
a barber	**o cabeleireiro de homens** *oo kuh • beh • lay • <u>ray</u> • roo deh <u>aw</u> • mengs*
a dry cleaner	**a lavandaria de limpeza a seco** *uh luh • vuhn • duh • <u>ree</u> • uh deh leeng • <u>peh</u> • zuh uh <u>seh</u> • koo*
a hairdresser	**o cabeleireiro de senhoras** *oo kuh • beh • lay • <u>ray</u> • roo deh see • <u>nyau</u> • ruhz*
a laundromat [launderette]	**a lavandaria** *uh luh • vuhn • duh • <u>ree</u> • uh*
a nail salon	**o salão das unhas** *oo suh • <u>lohm</u> duhz <u>oo</u> • nyuhz*
a spa	**o spa** *oo spa*
a travel agency	**a agência de viagens** *uh ah • <u>zsehn</u> • see • uh deh vee • <u>ah</u> • zsengs*
Can you…this?	**Pode…isto?** *pawd…<u>ee</u> • stoo*
alter	**modificar** *moo • dee • fee • <u>kahr</u>*
clean	**limpar** *leem • <u>parh</u>*
mend	**consertar** *kaun • sehr • <u>tahr</u>*
press	**engomar** *eeng • goo • <u>mahr</u>*
When will it be ready?	**Quando estará pronto?** *<u>kwuhn</u> • doo ee • stuh • <u>rah</u> <u>praun</u> • too*

HAIR & BEAUTY

I'd like…	**Queria…**
	keh • ree • uh…
an appointment	**fazer uma marcação**
for today/	**para hoje/amanhã**
tomorrow	*fuh • zehr oo • muh mahr • kuh • sohm*
	puh • ruh auzeh/uh • muh • nyuh
some color	**alguma cor**
	ahl • goo • muh kaur
some highlights	**madeixas**
	muh • day • shuhz
my hair styled/	**meu cabelo penteado/seco com secador**
blow-dried	*mehoo kuh • beh • loo pehn • tee • ah • thoo/*
	seh • koo kaum seh • kuh • daur
a haircut	**um corte**
	oong kawrt
a trim	**acertar as pontas**
	uh • sehr • tahr uhz paun • tuhz
Don't cut it too short.	**Não corte muito curto.**
	nohm kawrt mooee • too koor • too
Shorter here.	**Mais curto aqui.**
	meyez koor • too uh • kee
I'd like…	**Queria…**
	keh • ree • uh…
an eyebrow/	**uma cera de sobrancelha/biquíni**
a bikini wax	*oo • muh seh • ruh deh*
	sau • bruhn • seh • lyuhz/bee • kee • nee
I'd like…	**Queria…**
	keh • ree • uh…
a facial	**uma limpeza de pele**
	oo • muh leem • peh • zuh deh pehl

a manicure/ pedicure	**uma manicure/um pedicure** _oo • muh muh • nee • <u>koor</u>/oong peh • dee • <u>koor</u>_
a (sports) massage	**uma massagem (desportiva)** _oo • muh mehn • <u>sah</u> • zseng (dee • <u>spawr</u> • tee • vuh_
Do you do…?	**Faz…?** _fahz…_
acupuncture	**acupuntura** _uh • koo • poon • <u>too</u> • ruh_
aromatherapy	**aromaterapia** _uh • raw • muh • teh • reh • <u>pee</u> • uh_
oxygen treatment	**tratamento de oxigénio** _truh • tuh • <u>mehn</u> • too deh awk • see • <u>zseh</u> • nee • oo_
Is there a sauna?	**Há sauna?** _ah <u>sahoo</u> • nuh_

Portugal is well-known for the benefits of its natural mineral waters and offers many healing and wellness centers. Contact the **Associação das Termas de Portugal** (Association of Facilities of Portugal) for a list of centers throughout Portugal.
Check with your hotel concierge for information on local spas that offer massage, acupuncture and skin treatments. These spas are most often found in large cities. The service fee is usually included in the price, but an additional 10% tip is appreciated for extraordinary service.

ANTIQUES

How old is this?	**Qual é a data disto?** *kwahl eh uh dah • tuh dee • stoo*
Do you have anything from the period…?	**Tem alguma coisa do período…?** *teng ahl • goo • muh koy • zuh thoo peh • ree • oo • thoo…*
Do I have to fill out any forms?	**Tenho que completar algum formulário?** *teh • nyoo keh kaum • pleh • tahr ahl • goom fawr • moo • lah • ree • oo*
Is there a certificate of authenticity?	**Há um certificado de autenticidade?** *ah oong sehr • tee • fee • kah • thoo deh aw • tehn • tee • see • dahd*
Can you ship/ wrap it?	**Pode enviar/embrulhar?** *pawd ehn • vee • ahr/ehm • broo • lyahr*

CLOTHING

I'd like…	**Queria…**
	keh • ree • uh…
Can I try this on?	**Posso provar isto?**
	paw • soo proo • vahr ee • stoo
It doesn't fit.	**Não me serve.**
	nohm meh sehrv
It's too…	**É muito…**
	eh mooee • too…
big	**grande**
	grawnd
small	**pequeno** m/**pequena** f
	peh • kehn • oo/peh • kehn • uh
short	**curto** m/**curta** f
	koor • too/koor • tuh
long	**comprido** m/**comprida** f
	kaum • pree • doo/kaum • pree • duh
tight/loose	**justo/largo**
	zsooz • too/lahr • goo
Do you have this in size…?	**Tem isto no tamanho…?**
	teng ee • stoo noo tuh • muh • nyoo…

YOU MAY HEAR…

Isso fica-lhe bem.
ee • soo fee • kuh • lyeh beng

That looks great on you.

Como é que fica?
kau • moo eh keh fee • kuh

How does it fit?

Não temos o seu tamanho.
nohm teh • mooz oo sehoo tuh • muh • nyoo

We don't have your size.

Do you have this in a bigger/smaller size? **Tem isto num tamanho maior/mais pequeno?**

teng ee • stoo noong tuh • muh • nyoo meye • awr/meyez peh • kehn • oo

For Numbers, see page 20.

YOU MAY SEE...

ROUPA DE HOMEM	men's clothing
ROUPA DE SENHORA	women's clothing
ROUPA DE CRIANÇAS	children's clothing

COLORS

I'd like something... **Queria algo...**
keh • ree • uh ahl • goo...

beige
em beige
eng bay • zseh

black
em preto
eng preh • too

blue
em azul
eng uh • zool

brown
em castanho
eng kuhz • tay • nyoo

green
em verde
eng vehrd

gray
em cinzento
eng seeng • zehn • too [seen • zuh]

orange
em cor-de-laranja
eng kaur deh luh • ruhn • zsuh

pink	**em cor-de-rosa**
	eng kaur deh <u>raw</u> • zuh
purple	**em roxo**
	eng <u>rau</u> • shoo
red	**em vermelho**
	eng vehr • <u>meh</u> • lyoo
white	**em branco**
	eng <u>bruhn</u> • koo
yellow	**em amarelo**
	eng uh • meh • <u>reh</u> • loo

CLOTHES & ACCESSORIES

backpack	**a mochila**
	uh moo • <u>shee</u> • luh
belt	**o cinto**
	oo <u>seen</u> • too
bikini	**o bikini**
	oo bee • <u>kee</u> • nee
blouse	**a blusa**
	uh <u>bloo</u> • zuh
bra	**o soutien**
	oo soot • ee • <u>ehn</u>
briefs [underpants]	**as calcinhas**
	uhz kahl • <u>see</u> • nyuhz
coat	**o casaco comprido**
	oo kuh • <u>zah</u> • koo kaum • <u>pree</u> • thoo
dress	**o vestido**
	oo vehs • <u>tee</u> • thoo
hat	**o chapéu**
	oo shuh • <u>pehoo</u>
jacket	**o casaco curto**
	oo kuh • <u>zah</u> • koo <u>koor</u> • too
jeans	**as calças de ganga**
	uhz <u>kahl</u> • suhz deh <u>guhn</u> • guh

pants [trousers]	**as calças**
	uhz <u>kahl</u> • suhz
pantyhose [tights]	**o collant**
	oo koo • <u>luhnt</u>
purse [handbag]	**a mala de mão**
	uh <u>mah</u> • luh deh mohm
raincoat	**a gabardine**
	uh guh • buhr • <u>deen</u>
scarf	**o lenço de pescoço**
	oo <u>lehn</u> • soo deh pehz • <u>kau</u> • soo
shirt	**a camisa**
	uh kuh • <u>mee</u> • zuh
shorts	**os calções**
	ooz kahl • <u>soingz</u>
skirt	**a saia**
	uh <u>seye</u> • uh
socks	**as peúgas**
	uhz peh • <u>oo</u> • guhz
suit	**o fato**
	oo <u>fah</u> • too
sunglasses	**os óculos de sol**
	ooz <u>aw</u> • koo • looz deh sawl
sweater	**a camisola [o suéter]**
	uh kuh • mee • <u>zaw</u> • luh [oo <u>sweh</u> • tur]
sweatshirt	**o sweatshirt**
	oo <u>sweht</u> • shurt
swimming trunks	**os calções de banho**
	ooz kahl • <u>soingz</u> deh <u>buh</u> • nyoo
swimsuit	**o fato de banho**
	oo <u>fah</u> • too deh <u>buh</u> • nyoo
T-shirt	**a camiseta/T-shirt**
	uh kuh • mee • <u>seh</u> • tuh/tee • shurt
tie	**gravata**
	gruh • <u>vah</u> • tuh

underwear	**roupa interior**
	rau • puh eeng • teh • ree • _aur_

FABRIC

I'd like...	**Queria...**
	keh • _ree_ • uh...
cotton	**algodão**
	ahl • goo • _dohm_
denim	**ganga**
	guhn • guh
lace	**renda**
	rehn • duh
leather	**cabedal**
	kuh • beh • _dahl_
linen	**linho**
	lee • nyoo
silk	**seda**
	seh • thuh
wool	**lã**
	luh
Is it machine washable?	**Isto é para lavar na máquina?**
	_ee_ • stoo eh _puh_ • ruh luh • _vahr_ nuh _mah_ • kee • nuh

SHOES

I'd like a pair of...	**Queria um par de...**
	keh • _ree_ • uh oong pahr deh...
high-heeled/	**sapatos altos/baixos**
flat shoes	suh • _pah_ • tooz _ahl_ • tooz/ _beye_ • shooz
boots	**botas**
	baw • tuhz

loafers	**mandriões**	
	muhn • dree • <u>oingz</u>	
sandals	**sandálias**	
	suhn • <u>dah</u> • lee • uhz	
shoes	**sapatos**	
	suh • <u>pah</u> • tooz	
slippers	**chinelas**	
	shee • <u>neh</u> • luhz	
sneakers	**sapatos de ténis**	
	suh • <u>pah</u> • tooz deh <u>teh</u> • neez	
In size…	**No tamanho…**	
	noo tuh • <u>muh</u> • nyoo…	

For Numbers, see page 20.

SIZES

small (S)	**pequeno**	
	peh • <u>keh</u> • noo	
medium (M)	**medio**	
	<u>meh</u> • dee • oo	
large (L)	**grande**	
	gruhnd	
extra large (XL)	**extra grande**	
	<u>ay</u> • struh gruhnd	
petite	**pequeno**	
	peh • <u>keh</u> • noo	
plus size	**tamanho de factor positivo**	
	tuh • <u>muh</u> • nyoo deh <u>fah</u> • taur poo • see • <u>tee</u> • voo	

NEWSSTAND & TOBACCONIST

Do you sell English-language newspapers?	**Vende jornais em inglês?** *vehn • deh zsoor • neyez eng eeng • lehz*
I'd like…	**Queria…** *keh • ree • uh…*
candy [sweets]	**rebuçados** *reh • boo • sah • dooz*
chewing gum	**uma pastilha elástica** *oo • muh puhz • tee • lyuh ee • lah • stee • kuh*
a chocolate bar	**um chocolate** *oong shoo • koo • lah • teh*
a cigar	**um charuto** *oong shuh • roo • too*
I'd like…	**Queria…** *keh • ree • uh…*
a pack/carton of cigarettes	**um maço/pacote de cigarros** *oong mah • soo/ puh • kaut deh see • gah • rrooz*
a lighter	**um isqueiro** *oong ees • kay • roo*
a magazine	**uma revista** *oo • muh reh • vee • stuh*
matches	**fósforos** *fawz • fuh • rooz*
a newspaper	**um jornal** *oong zsoorr • nahl*
a pen	**uma caneta** *oo • muh kuh • neh • tuh*
a postcard	**um postal** *oong poo • stahl*

a road/town	**um mapa de/da cidade de...**
map of...	*oong <u>mah</u> • puh*
	deh/deh <u>see</u> • dahd deh...
stamps	**selos**
	<u>seh</u> • looz

PHOTOGRAPHY

I'm looking for...	**Estou à procura de uma**
camera.	**máquina fotográfica...**
	ee • <u>stawoo</u> ah praw • <u>koo</u> • ruh
	deh <u>oo</u> • muh <u>mah</u> • kee • nuh
	faw • too • <u>grah</u> • fee • kuh...
an automatic	**automática**
	<u>ahoo</u> • too • <u>mah</u> • tee • kuh
a digital	**digital**
	deh • zseh • <u>tahl</u>
a disposable	**descartável**
	dehz • kuhr • <u>tah</u> • vehl
I'd like...	**Queria...**
	keh • <u>ree</u> • uh...
a battery	**uma pilha**
	<u>oo</u> • muh <u>pee</u> • lyuh

digital prints	**impressões digitais**
	eem • preh • <u>soingz</u> deh • zseh • <u>teyez</u>
a memory card	**um cartão de memória**
	oong kuhr • <u>tohm</u> deh meh • <u>maw</u> • ree • uh
Can I print digital photos here?	**Posso imprimir fotos digitais aqui?**
	<u>paw</u> • soo eem • pree • <u>meer faw</u> • tooz deh • zeh • <u>teyez</u> uh • <u>kee</u>

SOUVENIRS

bottle of wine	**a garrafa de vinho**
	uh guh • <u>rrah</u> • fuh deh <u>vee</u> • nyoo
box of chocolates	**a caixa de chocolates**
	uh <u>keye</u> • shuh deh shoo • koo • <u>lah</u> • tehz
calendar	**o calendário**
	oo kuh • lehn • <u>dah</u> • ree • oo
postcards	**postais**
	pooz • <u>teyez</u>
scarf	**o lenço**
	oo <u>lehn</u> • soo
souvenir guide	**o guia turístico**
	oo <u>gee</u> • uh too • <u>ree</u> • stee • koo
T-shirt	**a camiseta**
	uh kuh • mee • <u>seh</u> • tuh
toy/game	**o brinquedo/jogo**
	oo breeng • <u>keh</u> • thoo/<u>zsaw</u> • goo
wine	**o vinho**
	oo <u>vee</u> • nyoo
Can I see this/that?	**Posso ver este/esse?**
	<u>paw</u> • soo vehr ehst/eh • seh
It's the one in the window/display case.	**É aquele na janela/montra.**
	eh uh • <u>kehl</u> nuh zsuh • <u>neh</u> • luh/ <u>mau</u> • ntruh
I'd like…	**Queria…**
	keh • <u>ree</u> • uh…

a battery	**uma pilha**
	_oo_ • muh _pee_ • lyuh
a bracelet	**uma pulseira**
	_oo_ • muh pool • _say_ • ruh
a brooch	**um broche**
	oong brawsh
earrings	**uns brincos**
	oongs _breeng_ • kooz
a necklace	**um colar**
	oong koo • _lahr_
a ring	**um anel**
	oong uh • _nehl_
a watch	**um relógio de pulso**
	oong reh • _loy_ • zsoo deh _pool_ • soo
copper	**cobre**
	kaw • breh
crystal	**cristal**
	kree • _stahl_
diamonds	**brilhantes**
	bree • _lyuhntz_
white/yellow gold	**ouro branco/amarelo**
	_au_ • roo _bruhn_ • koo/uh • muh • _reh_ • loo
pearls	**pérolas**
	peh • roo • luhz
pewter	**peltre**
	pehl • treh
platinum	**platina**
	plah • tee • nuh
sterling silver	**prata**
	prah • tuh
Is this real?	**É verdadeiro?**
	eh vehr • duh • _day_ • roo
Can you engrave it?	**Pode gravá-lo?**
	pawd gruh • _vah_ • loo

Some souvenirs that you might want to take home from Portugal include hand-painted pottery, leather sandals, belts, bags, gloves and the like, tiles and copperware, especially the famous **cataplana** (copper seafood pot). Wooden painted roosters (**galos de barcelos**) also make great souvenirs as they are a national symbol. Products made out of cork are also really popular and you can find anything from bath mats to place mats and ornaments made out of cork tiles. Alternatively, a bottle of the famous **Vinho do Porto**, Port wine will usually be well-received.

SPORT & LEISURE

NEED TO KNOW

When's the game?	**Quando é o jogo?**
	kwuhn • doo eh o zsau • goo
Where's…?	**Onde é…?**
	aund eh…
the beach	**a praia**
	uh preye • uh
the park	**o parque**
	oo pahr • keh
the pool	**a piscina**
	uh pee • see • nuh
Is it safe to swim here?	**Pode-se nadar aqui sem perigo?**
	pawd seh nuh • dahr uh • kee sehn peh • ree • goo

Can I hire golf clubs?	**Posso alugar tacos?**
	paw • soo uh • loo • gahr tah • kooz
How much per hour?	**Qual é a tarifa por hora?**
	kwahl eh uh tuh • ree • fuh poor aw • ruh
How far is it to…?	**A que distância fica…?**
	uh keh dee • stuhn • see • uh fee • kuh…
Can you show me on the map?	**Pode indicar-me no mapa?**
	pawd een • dee • kahr • meh noo mah • puh

WATCHING SPORT

When's…?	**Quando é…?**
	kwuhn • doo eh…
the basketball game	**o jogo de basquetebol**
	oo zsau • goo deh bah • skeht • bawl
the boxing match	**a partida de boxe**
	uh puhr • tee • duh deh bawkz
the cycling race	**a corrida de bicicleta**
	uh koo • ree • thuh deh bee • see • kleht
the golf tournament	**o torneio de golfe**
	oo taur • nay • oo deh gawlf
the soccer [football] game	**o jogo de futebol**
	oo zsau • goo deh foo • teh • bawl
When's…?	**Quando é…?**
	kwuhn • doo eh…
the basketball game	**o jogo de basquetebol**
	oo zsau • goo deh bah • skeht • bawl
the tennis match	**a partida de ténis**
	uh puhr • tee • thuh de teh • neez
the volleyball game	**o jogo de voleibol**
	oo zsau • goo deh vaw • lay • bawl

Which teams are playing?	**Quais são as equipas que jogam?**
	kweyez sohm uhz ee • kee • puhz keh zsau • gohm
Where's…?	**Onde é…?**
	aund eh…
the horsetrack	**a pista de cavalo**
	uh peez • tuh deh kuh • vah • loo
the racetrack	**o hipódromo**
	oo ee • paw • drau • moo
the stadium	**o pavilhão desportivo**
	oo puh • vee • lyohm dehs • poor • tee • voo
Where can I place a bet?	**Onde posso colocar uma aposta?**
	aund paw • soo kaw • loo • kahr oo • muh uh • paws • tuh

i

The Portuguese are avid soccer fans. In Portugal, the teams Benfica, Porto and Sporting Lisbon attract huge crowds and nights when a live game is playing are always a lively evening out.

PLAYING SPORT

Where's…?	**Onde é…?**
	aund eh…
the golf course	**o campo de golfe**
	oo kuhm • poo deh gawlf
the gym	**o clube desportivo**
	oo kloob dehs • poor • tee • voo
the park	**o parque**
	oo pahrk

the tennis courts	**os campos de ténis**
	ooz kuhm • pooz deh teh • neez
How much per…?	**Qual é o preço por…?**
	kwahl eh oo preh • soo poor…
day	**dia**
	dee • uh
hour	**hora**
	aw • ruh
game	**jogo**
	zsau • goo
round	**volta**
	vawl • tuh
Can I rent [hire]…?	**Posso alugar…?**
	paw • soo uh • loo • gahr…
golf clubs	**tacos de golfe**
	tah • kooz deh gawlf
equipment	**o equipamento**
	oo ee • kee • puh • mehn • too
a racket	**uma raquete**
	oo • muh rah • keht

AT THE BEACH/POOL

Where's the beach/pool?	**Onde é a praia/piscina?** *aund eh uh <u>preye</u> • uh/pee • <u>see</u> • nuh*
Is there…?	**Há…?** *ah…*
a kiddie pool	**uma piscina para crianças** *<u>oo</u> • muh pee • <u>see</u> • nuh <u>puh</u> • ruh kree • <u>uhn</u> • suhs*
an indoor/outdoor pool	**uma piscina coberta/ao ar livre** *<u>oo</u> • muh pee • <u>see</u> • nuh koo • <u>behr</u> • tuh/ahoo ahr lee • vreh*
a lifeguard	**uma salva-vidas** *<u>oo</u> • muh <u>sahl</u> • vuh <u>vee</u> • duhz*
Is it safe…?	**É perigoso…?** *eh per • ree • gau • zoo…*
to swim	**para nadar** *<u>puh</u> • ruh nuh • <u>dahr</u>*
to dive	**para mergulhar** *<u>puh</u> • ruh mehr • goo • <u>lyahr</u>*
for children	**para as crianças** *<u>puh</u> • ruh uhz kree • <u>uhn</u> • suhs*
I want to hire…	**Quero alugar…** *<u>keh</u> • roo uh • loo • <u>gahr</u>…*
a deck chair	**uma cadeira de encosto** *<u>oo</u> • muh kuh • <u>day</u> • ruh deh ehn • <u>kaus</u> • stoo*
diving equipment	**equipamento para mergulhar** *ee • kee • puh • <u>mehn</u> • too <u>puh</u> • ruh mehr • goo • <u>lyahr</u>*
a jet-ski	**um jet-ski** *oong <u>zseht</u> • skee*
a motorboat	**um barco a motor** *oong <u>bahr</u> • koo uh moo • <u>taur</u>*

a rowboat	**um barco a remos**
	oong bahr • koo uh reh • mooz
snorkling equipment	**equipamento de snorkling**
	ee • kee • puh • mehn • too de snawr • kleeng
a surfboard	**uma prancha de surf**
	oo • muh pruhn • shuh deh soorf
a towel	**uma toalha**
	oo • muh too • ah • lyuh
an umbrella	**um chapéu de sol**
	oong shuh • pehoo deh sol
water skis	**esquis-aquáticos**
	eez • keez uh • kwah • tee • kooz
a windsurfer	**uma prancha à vela**
	oo • muh pruhn • shuh ah veh • luh
For…hours.	**Por…horas.**
	poor…aw • ruhz

For Traveling with Children, see page 136.

ℹ

The **Algarve** area in the south is home to many beautiful beaches, although it can become crowded with tourists in the summer months. The wilder **Alentejo** (Atlantic Coast) is also popular but quieter. Meanwhile, the beaches in the north (**Caminha**, **Apúlia**, **Furadouro**) offer good surfing.
The main and bigger beaches will have lifeguards on duty during peak periods, but always look for the following swimming flags before going into the water: red (swimming forbidden), yellow (swim near the beach), green (safe to swim).

WINTER SPORTS

A lift pass for a day/ five days, please.	**Uma passagem de esqui por um dia/ cinco dias, por favor.** _oo • muh puh • sah • zseng deh ee • skee poor oong dee • uh/seeng • koo dee • uhz poor fuh • vaur_
I want to hire…	**Quero alugar…** _keh • roo uh • loo • gahr…_
boots	**botas** _baw • tuhz_
a helmet	**um capacete** _oong kuh • puh • seht_
poles	**polos** _pau • looz_
skis	**esquis** _ee • skeez_
a snowboard	**um snowboard** _oong sno • bawrd_
snowshoes	**sapatos de neve** _suh • pah • tooz deh nehv_
These are too big/ small.	**Estes são muito grandes/pequenos.** _ehs • tehz sohm mooee • too gruhn • dehz/ pee • keh • nooz_
Are there lessons?	**Há lições?** _ah lee • soingz_
I'm a beginner.	**Sou principiante.** _sawoo preen • see • puhnt_
I'm experienced.	**Tenho experiência.** _teh • nyoo ees • peh • ree • ehn • see • uh_
A trail [piste] map, please.	**Um mapa de trilha, por favor.** _oong mah • puh deh tree • lyuh poor fuh • vaur_

There is one place in Portugal with temperatures cold enough for skiing: **Serra da Estrela**, Portugal's highest mountain. Dress appropriately, as the weather at the bottom of the mountain (and the rest of Portugal) is not indicative of the freezing temperatures at the top of **Serra da Estrela**. It is not uncommon for temperatures to be thirty to fifty degrees colder at the top!

YOU MAY SEE...

LEVANTA DE ESQUI	drag lift
CARRO DE CABO/GANDOLA	cable car/gondola
CADEIRA LEVANTAMENTO	chair lift
NOVATO	novice
INTERMEDIÁRIO	intermediate
ESPECIALISTA	expert
PISTA FECHADA	trail [piste] closed

OUT IN THE COUNTRY

I'd like a map...	**Queria um mapa...** *keh • ree • uh oong mah • puh...*
of this region	**desta região** *deh • stuh reh • zsee • ohm*
of the walking routes	**de itinerários a pé** *deh ee • tee • neh • rah • ree • ooz a peh*

of bike routes	**de itinerários de bicicleta**
	deh ee • tee • neh • <u>rah</u> • ree • ooz deh bee • see • <u>kleh</u> • tuh
of the trails	**dos caminhos**
	thooz kuh • <u>mee</u> • nyooz
Is it easy/difficult ?	**É fácil/difícil?**
	eh <u>fah</u> • seel/dee <u>fee</u> • seel
Is it far/steep?	**É distante/precipício?**
	eh deez • <u>tuhnt</u>/pree • see • <u>pee</u> • see • oo
How far is it to…?	**A que distância fica…**
	uh keh dee • <u>stuhn</u> • see • uh <u>fee</u> • kuh…
Can you show me on the map?	**Pode indicar-me no mapa?**
	pawd een • dee • <u>kahr</u> • meh noo <u>mah</u> • puh
I'm lost.	**Estou perdido** *m /***perdida** *f.*
	ee • <u>stawoo</u> pehr • <u>dee</u> • doo/ pehr • <u>dee</u> • duh
Where's…?	**Onde é…?**
	aund eh…
the bridge	**a ponte**
	uh paunt
the cave	**a caverna**
	uh kuh • <u>vehr</u> • nuh
the cliff	**a falésia**
	uh fuh • <u>leh</u> • see • uh
the desert	**o deserto**
	oo deh • <u>zehr</u> • too
the farm	**a quinta**
	uh <u>keen</u> • tuh
the field	**o campo**
	oo <u>kuhm</u> • poo
the forest	**a floresta**
	uh flau • <u>reh</u> • stuh
the hill	**a colina**
	uh koo • <u>lee</u> • nuh

the lake	**o lago** *oo lah • goo*
the mountain	**a montanha** *uh maun • tah • nyuh*
the nature preserve	**a reserva natural** *uh reh • zehr • vuh nuh • too • rahl*
the view point	**o miradouro** *oo mee • ruh • dau • roo*
the park	**o parque** *oo pahrk*
the path	**o caminho para peões** *oo kuh • mee • nyoo puh • ruh pee • oingz*
the peak	**o pico** *oo pee • koo*
the picnic area	**a área de piqueniques** *a ahr • ee • uh deh pee • keh • nee • kehz*
the pond	**a lagoa** *uh luh • gaw • uh*
the river	**o rio** *oo rree • oo*
the sea	**o mar** *oo mahr*
the valley	**o vale** *oo vahl*
Where's…?	**Onde é…?** *aund eh…*
the vineyard	**a vinha** *uh vee • nyuh*
the waterfall	**a cascata** *uh kuhz • kah • tuh*

For Souvenirs, see page 124.

TRAVELING WITH CHILDREN

NEED TO KNOW

Is there a discount for children?	**Há desconto para crianças?** *ah dehs • caun • too puh • ruh kree • uhn • suhs*
Can you recommend a babysitter?	**Pode recomendar-me uma babysitter qualificada?** *pawd reh • koo • mehn • dahr • meh oo • muh bay • bee • sit • tur kwahl • ee • fee • kah • duh*
Do you have a child's seat?	**Pode trazer uma cadeirinha de criança?** *pawd truh • zehr oo • muh kuh • day • ree • nyuh deh kree • uhn • suh*
Where can I change the baby?	**Onde posso mudar o bebé?** *aund paw • soo moo • dahr oo beh • beh*

OUT & ABOUT

Can you recommend something for the kids?	**Pode recomendar-me algo próprio para crianças?**
	pawd reh • koo • mehn • _dahr_ • meh _ahl_ • goo _praw_ • pree • oo _puh_ • ruh kree • _uhn_ • suhs
Where's…?	**Onde é…?**
	aund eh…
the amusement park	**o parque de diversões**
	oo _pahr_ • keh deh dee • vehr • _sohmz_
the arcade park	**o salão de jogos**
	oo suh • _lohm_ deh _zsaw_ • gooz
the kiddie [paddling] pool	**a piscina de bebés**
	uh pee • _see_ • nuh deh beh • _behz_
the park	**o parque**
	oo pahrk
the playground	**o parque de recreio**
	oo pahrk deh reh • _kray_ • oo
the zoo	**o jardim zoológico**
	oo zsuhr • _deem_ zoo • _law_ • zsee • koo
Are kids allowed?	**São permitidas crianças?**
	sohm pehr • mee • _tee_ • thuhz kree • _uhn_ • suhs
Is it safe for kids?	**É seguro para as crianças?**
	eh seh • _goo_ • roo puh • ruh uhz kree • _uhn_ • suhs
Is it suitable for… year olds?	**Será bom para crianças com…anos?**
	seh • _rah_ bohng puh • ruh kree • _uhn_ • suhz kaum…_uh_ • nooz

For Numbers, see page 20.

YOU MAY HEAR...

Que giro!	How cute!
keh zsee • roo	
O que é o nome dele/dela?	What's his/her
oo kee eh oo nau • meh dehl/deh • luh	name?
Quantos anos tem ele/ela?	How old is he/
kwuh • tooz uh • nooz teng ehl/eh • luh	she?

BABY ESSENTIALS

Do you have…? **Tem…?**
teng…

a baby bottle **um biberom**
oong bee • brohng

baby wipes **os toalhetes de limpeza para o bebé**
ooz too • ah • lyehtz deh leem • peh • zuh puh • ruh oo beh • beh

a car seat **um assento de carro**
oong uh • sehn • too deh kah • rroo

a children's menu/ **uma ementa/dose de criança**
portion *oo • muh ee • mehn • tuh/daw • zeh deh kree • uhn • suh*

a child's seat **uma cadeirinha de criança**
oo • muh kuh • day • ree • nyuh deh kree • uhn • suh

a crib **uma cama de bebé**
oo • muh kuh • muh deh beh • beh

diapers [nappies] **as fraldas**
uhz frahl • duhz

formula **fórmula de bebé**
fawr • moo • luh deh beh • beh

a pacifier [dummy]	**uma chupeta**
	oo • muh shoo • peh • tuh
a playpen	**um parque para crianças**
	oong pahr • kuh puh • ruh kree • uhn • suhz
a stroller	**uma cadeira de bebé**
[pushchair]	*oo • muh kuh • day • ruh deh beh • beh*
Can I breastfeed the baby here?	**Posso amamentar o bebé aqui?**
	paw • soo uh • muh • mehn • tahr oo beh • beh uh • kee
Where can I change the baby?	**Onde posso mudar o bebé?**
	aund paw • soo moo • thahr oo beh • beh

For Dining with Children, see page 173.

BABYSITTING

Can you recommend a reliable babysitter?	**Pode recomendar-me uma babysitter qualificada?**
	pawd reh • koo • mehn • dahr • meh oo • muh bay • bee • sit • tur kwah • lee • fee • kah • thuh
What's the charge?	**Qual é o preço?**
	kwahl eh oo preh • soo
I'll be back by…	**Volto às…**
	vawl • too ahz…
I can be reached at…	**Pode-me encontrar…**
	pawd • meh ng • kaun • trahr…

For Time, see page 23.

SAFE TRAVEL

EMERGENCIES	142
POLICE	144
HEALTH	147
PHARMACY	154
DISABLED TRAVELERS	160

EMERGENCIES

NEED TO KNOW

Help!	**Socorro!**
	soo • kau • rroo
Go away!	**Vá-se embora!**
	vah • seh ehng • baw • ruh
Call the police!	**Chame a polícia!**
	shuh • meh uh poo • lee • see • uh
Stop thief!	**Pára ladrão!**
	pah • ruh luh • drohm
Get a doctor!	**Chame um médico!**
	shuh • meh oong meh • dee • koo
Fire!	**Fogo!**
	fau • goo
I'm lost.	**Estou perdido** *m*/**perdida** *f.*
	ee • stawoo pehr • dee • thoo/
	pehr • dee • thuh
Can you help me?	**Pode ajudar-me?**
	pawd uh • zsoo • dahr • meh

POLICE

YOU MAY HEAR...

Preencha este formulário.
pree • eng • sheh eh • stuh
fawr • muh • lah • reeoo

Fill out this form.

A sua identificação, por favor.
uh soo • uh
ee • dehnt • tee • fee • kuh • sohm
por fuh • vaur

Your identification, please.

Quando/Onde é que foi?
kwuhn • doo/aund eh keh foy

When/Where did it happen?

Como é ele/ela?
kau • moo eh ehleh/ehluh

What does he/she look like?

In Portugal, in an emergency dial **112** for the police, ambulance or fire brigade.

CRIME & LOST PROPERTY

NEED TO KNOW

Call the police!	**Chame a polícia!** _shuh_ • meh uh poo • _lee_ • see • uh
Where's the police station?	**Onde é a esquadra da polícia?** _aund_ eh uh ee • _skwahr_ • duh thuh poo • _lee_ • see • uh
There has been an accident/attack.	**Houve um acidente/ataque.** _auoo_ • veh oong uh • see • _dehnt_/uh • _tah_ • keh
My son/daughter is missing.	**O meu filho/A minha filha desapareceu.** oo mehoo _fee_ • lyoo/uh mee • nyuh _fee_ • lyuh deh • zuh • puh • ruh • _seoo_
I need...	**Preciso de...** preh • _see_ • zoo deh...
an interpreter	**um tradutor** oong truh • doo • _taur_
I need...	**Preciso de...** preh • _see_ • zoo deh...
to contact my lawyer	**contactar o meu advogado** kaun • tuhk • _tahr_ oo mehoo uhd • voo • _gah_ • thoo
to make a phone call	**fazer um telefonema** fuh • _zehr_ oong teh • leh • foo • _neh_ • muh
I'm innocent.	**Sou inocente.** sawoo ee • naw • _sehnt_

I want to report…	**Quero reportar…**
	keh • roo reh • paur • tahr…
a mugging	**um assalto**
	oong uh • sahl • too
a rape	**uma violação**
	oo • muh vee • au • luh • sohm
a theft	**um roubo**
	oong rau • boo
I've been robbed.	**Fui roubado** *m*/**roubada** *f.*
	fooee raw • bah • thoo/raw • bah • thuh
I've been mugged.	**Fui assaltado** *m*/**assaltada** *f.*
	fooee uh • sahl • tah • thoo/ uh • sahl • tah • duh
I've lost my…	**Perdi…**
	pehr • thee…
My…has/have been stolen.	**Roubaram-me…**
	raw • bah • rohm • meh…
backpack	**a mochila**
	uh moo • sheeh • luh
bicycle	**a bicicleta**
	uh bee • see • kleh • tuh
camera	**a máquina fotográfica**
	uh mah • kee • nuh faw • too • grah • fee • kuh
(hire) car	**o carro (alugado)**
	oo kah • rroo (uh • loo • gah • doo)
computer	**o computador**
	oo kaum • poo • tuh • daur
credit card	**os cartão de crédito**
	ooz kuhr • tohm deh kreh • dee • too
jewelry	**as jóias**
	uhz zsoy • uhz
money	**o dinheiro**
	oo dee • nyay • roo

passport	**o passaporte**
	oo pah • suh • <u>pawrt</u>
purse [handbag]	**a carteira**
	uh kuhr • <u>tay</u> • truh
traveler's checks [cheques]	**os cheques de viagem.**
	ooz shehkz deh vee • <u>ah</u> • zseng
wallet	**a carteira (de documentos)**
	uh kuhr • <u>tay</u> • ruh (deh doo • koo • <u>mehn</u> • tooz)
I need a police report.	**Preciso de um documento da policia.**
	preh • <u>see</u> • zoo deh oong thoo • koo • <u>mehn</u> • too duh poo • <u>lee</u> • see • uh
Where is the British/ American/Irish embassy?	**Onde fica a embaixada Britânica/ Americana/Irlandesa?**
	aund fee • kuh uh ehm • beye • shah • duh bree • tuhn • nee • kuh/ uh • meh • ree • kuh • nuh/ eer • luhn • deh • zuh

HEALTH

NEED TO KNOW

I'm sick [ill].	**Estou doente.**
	ee • stawoo doo • ehnt
I need an English-speaking doctor.	**Preciso de um médico que fale inglês.**
	preh • see • zoo deh oong meh • dee • koo keh fah • leh eeng • lehz
It hurts here.	**Dói-me aqui.**
	doy • meh uh • kee
I have a stomachache.	**Tenho uma dor de estômago.**
	teh • nyoo oo • muh daur deh ee • stau • muh • goo

FINDING A DOCTOR

Can you recommend a doctor/dentist?	**Pode recomendar um médico/dentista?**
	pawd reh • koo • mehn • dahr oong meh • dee • koo/dehn • teeh • stuh
Could the doctor come to see me here?	**O médico podia vir cá ver-me?**
	oo meh • dee • koo poo • thee • uh veer kah vehr • meh
I need an English-speaking doctor.	**Preciso de um médico que fale inglês.**
	preh • see • zoo deh oong meh • dee • koo keh fah • leh eeng • lehz
What are the office hours?	**A que horas é que há consulta?**
	uh kee aw • ruhz eh keh ah kaun • sool • tuh

I'd like to make an appointment…
Queria marcar uma consulta…
keh • ree • uh muhr • kahr oo • muh kaun • sool • tuh…

for today
para hoje
puh • ruh auyzseh

for tomorrow
para amanhã
puh • ruh uh • muh • nyuh

as soon as possible
o mais cedo possível
oo meyez seh • thoo poo • see • vel

It's urgent.
É urgente.
eh oor • zsehnt

YOU MAY HEAR…

Qual é o problema?
kwahl eh oo proo • bleh • muh
What's the problem?

Onde é que lhe dói?
aund eh keh lyeh doy
Where does it hurt?

Dói-lhe aqui?
doy • lyeh uh • kee
Does it hurt here?

Toma medicamentos?
taw • muh meh • dee • kuh • mehn • tooz
Are you on medication?

É alérgico m/alérgica f a algo?
eh uh • lehr • zsee • koo/
uh • lehr • zsee • kuh uh ahl • goo
Are you allergic to anything?

Abra a boca.
ah • bruh uh bau • kuh
Open your mouth.

Respire fundo.
rehs • pee • reh foon • doo
Breathe deeply.

Tussa, por favor.
too • suh, poor fuh • vaur
Cough, please.

Quero que vá para o hospital.
keh • roo keh vah puh • ruh oo aws • pee • tahl
I want you to go to the hospital.

SYMPTOMS

I'm...	**Estou...**
	ee • stawoo...
bleeding	**a sangrar**
	uh suhn • grahr
constipated	**constipado** m/**constipada** f
	kaun • stee • pah • thoo/
	kaun • stee • pah • thuh
dizzy	**com a cabeça à roda**
	kaum uh kuh • beh • suh ah raw • thuh
I'm nauseous.	**Estou enjoado** m/**enjoada** f.
	ee • stawoo eng • zsoo • ah • thoo/
	eng • zsoo • ah • thuh
I'm vomiting.	**Estou a vomitar.**
	ee • stawoo uh voo • mee • tahr
It hurts here.	**Dói-me aqui.**
	doy • meh uh • kee
I have...	**Tenho...**
	teh • nyoo...
an allergic reaction	**uma reacção alérgica**
	oo • muh rree • ah • sohm
	uh • lehr • gee • kuh
chest pain	**dor de peito**
	daur deh pay • too
diarrhea	**diarreia**
	dee • uh • rray • uh
an earache	**dor de ouvidos**
	daur deh aw • vee • thooz
a fever	**uma febre**
	oo • muh feh • breh
pain	**dor**
	daur

a rash	**uma erupção cutânea**
	_oo_ • muh eer • oop • _sohm_
	koo • _tuh_ • nee • uh
a sprain	**uma distensão muscular**
	_oo_ • muh dees • tehn • _sohm_
	moos • koo • lahr
some swelling	**algum inchaço**
	ahl • goong een • _shah_ • soo
a stomachache	**dor de estômago**
	daur deh ee • _stau_ • muh • goo
I have sunstroke.	**Apanhei uma insolação.**
	uh • puh • _nyay oo_ • muh
	een • soo • luh • _sohm_
I've been sick [ill]	**Há...dias que me sinto doente.**
for...days.	ah..._dee_ • uhz keh meh _seen_ • too
	doo • _ehnt_

For Numbers, see page 20.

CONDITIONS

I'm...	**Sou...**
	sawoo...
anemic	**anémico** m/**anémica** f
	uh • _neh_ • mee • koo/uh • _neh_ • mee • kuh
asthmatic	**asmático** m/**asmática** f
	uhz • _mah_ • tee • koo/uhz • _mah_ • tee • kuh
diabetic	**diabético** m/**diabética** f
	dee • uh • _beh_ • tee • koo/
	dee • uh • _beh_ • tee • kuh
epileptic	**epiléptico**
	eh • pee • leh • tee • koo

I'm allergic to antibiotics/ penicillin.	**Sou alérgico** m/**alérgica** f **a antibióticos penicilina.**
	sawoo uh • lehr • gee • koo/ uh • lehr • gee • kuh uh uhn • tee • bee • aw • tee • kuhz/ peh • neh • seh • lee • nuh
I have arthritis.	**Tenho artrite.**
	teh • nyoo uh • treet
I have a heart condition.	**Tenho um problema de coração.**
	teh • nyoo oong proo • bleh • muh deh koo • ruh • sohm
I have high/low low blood pressure.	**Tenho a pressão arterial alta/baixa.**
	teh • nyoo uh preh • sohm uhr • teh • ree • ahl ahl • tuh/beye • shuh
I'm on…	**Estou em…**
	ee • stawoo eng…

TREATMENT

Do I need medicine?	**Preciso de algum medicamento?**
	preh • see • zoo deh ahl • goong meh • dee • kuh • mehn • too
Can you prescribe a generic drug [unbranded medication]?	**Pode prescrever um medicamento genérico?**
	pawd prehz • kreh • vehr oong meh • dee • kuh • mehn • too geh • neh • ree • koo
Where can I get it?	**Onde posso obtê-lo?**
	aund paw • soo au • bteh • loo

For What to Take, see page 155.

HOSPITAL

Please notify my family.
Por favor informe a minha família.
poor fuh • vaur eeng • fawr • meh uh mee • nyuh fuh • mee • lyuh

I'm in pain.
Estou com dores.
ee • stawoo kaun daur • ehz

I need a doctor/ nurse.
Necessito um médico/uma enfermeira.
neh • seh • see • too oong meh • dee • koo • oo • muh een • fehr • may • ruh

When are visiting hours?
Quais são as horas de visitas?
kweyez sohm uhz aw • ruhz deh vee • zee • tuhz

I'm visiting…
Estou a visitar…
ee • stawoo uh vee • see • tahr…

DENTIST

I've broken a tooth/ lost a filling.
Parti um dente./Perdi um chumbo.
pehr • thee oong dehnt/pehr • thee oong shoom • boo

I have a toothache.
Tenho dor de dentes.
teh • nyoo daur deh dehntz

Can you fix this denture?
Pode consertar esta dentadura?
pawd kaun • sehr • tahr eh • stuh dehn • tuh • doo • ruh

GYNECOLOGIST

I have menstrual cramps/a vaginal infection.
Tenho dores de períodos menstruais/ uma infecção na vagina.
teh • nyoo daurz duh pehr • ree • oo • thooz mehn • stroo • eyez/oo • muh eeng • feh • sohm nuh vuh • zsee • nuh

I missed my period.	**Faltou-me o meu período.** *fahl • tawoo • meh oo meeoo* *peh • ree • oo • thoo*
I'm on the pill.	**Estou a tomar a pílula.** *ee • stawoo uh too • mar uh pee • loo • luh*
I'm (not) pregnant.	**(Não) Estou grávida.** *(nohm) ee • stawoo grah • vee • thuh*
I haven't had my period for…months.	**Já não tenho o meu período há…meses.** *zsah nohm teh • nyoo oo mehoo* *peh • ree • oo • thoo ah…meh • zehz*

OPTICIAN

I've lost…	**Perdi…** *pehr • thee…*
one of my contact lenses	**uma das minhas lentes de contacto** *oo • muh duhz mee • nyuhz lehn • tehz deh* *kaun • tahk • too*
my glasses	**os meus óculos** *ooz mehooz aw • koo • looz*
a lens	**uma lente** *oo • muh lehnt*

PAYMENT & INSURANCE

How much?	**Quanto é?** *kwuhn • too eh*
Can I pay by credit card?	**Posso pagar com cartão de crédito?** *paw • soo puh • gahr kaum oo kuhr • tohm* *deh kreh • dee • too*
I have insurance.	**Tenho seguro.** *teh • nyoo seh • goo • roo*

Can you give me a receipt for my health insurance?

Pode dar-me um recibo para o meu seguro de saúde?

pawd dar • meh oong reh • see • boo puh • ruh oo mehoo seh • goo • roo deh suh • oo • theh

PHARMACY

NEED TO KNOW

Where's the pharmacy [chemist]?

Onde fica a farmácia?

aund fee • kuh uh fuhr • mah • see • uh

What time does the pharmacy open/close?

A que horas é que a farmácia abre/fecha?

uh keh aw • ruhz eh keh uh fuhr • mah • see • uh ah • breh/feh • shuh

What would you recommend for…?

O que é que me recomenda para…?

oo keh eh keh meh reh • koo • mehn • duh puh • ruh…

How much should I take?	**Quanto é que devo tomar?** _kwuhn • too eh keh <u>deh</u> • voo too • <u>mahr</u>_
Can you fill [make up] this prescription for	**Pode aviar-me esta receita?** _pawd uh • vee • <u>ahr</u> • meh eh • stuh reh • <u>say</u> • tuh_
I'm allergic to…	**Sou alérgico m/alérgica f a…** _sawoo uh • <u>lehr</u> • zsee • koo/ uh • <u>lehr</u> • zsee • kuh ah…_

WHAT TO TAKE

How much should I take?	**Quanto é que devo tomar?** _kwuhn • too eh keh <u>deh</u> • voo too • <u>mahr</u>_
How often should I take it?	**Quantas vezes é que devo tomar?** _kwuhn • tuhz <u>veh</u> • zehz eh keh <u>deh</u> • voo too • <u>mahr</u>_
Is it suitable for children?	**É próprio para crianças?** _eh <u>praw</u> • pree • oo <u>puh</u> • ruh kree • <u>uhn</u> • suhs_
I'm taking…	**Estou a tomar…** _ee • <u>stawoo</u> uh too • <u>mahr</u>…_
Are there side effects?	**Há efeitos colaterais?** _ah ee • <u>fay</u> • tooz kaw • <u>luh</u> • tehr • eyez_
I'd like some medicine for…	**Queria um remédio para…** _keh • <u>ree</u> • uh oohn ruh • meh • <u>dee</u> • oo <u>puh</u> • ruh…_
a cold	**uma constipação** _<u>oo</u> • muh kaun • stee • puh • <u>sohm</u>_
a cough	**a tosse** _uh <u>taw</u> • seh_

diarrhea	**a diarreia**
	uh dee • uh • rray • uh
a headache	**uma dor de cabeça**
	oo • muh daur deh kuh • beh • suh
insect bites	**as picadas de insecto**
	uhz pee • kah • duhz deh eeng • sehk • too
motion sickness	**o enjoo**
	oo ehn • zsau • oo
a sore throat	**a dor de garganta**
	uh daur deh guhr • guhn • tuh
sunburn	**uma queimadura de sol**
	oo • muh kay • muh • doo • ruh deh sawl
a toothache	**uma dor de dentes**
	oo • muh daur deh dehnts
an upset stomach	**uma indisposição gástrica**
	oo • muh een • dees • poo • zee • sohm gahz • tree • kuh

Pharmacies are easily recognized by their sign: a green or red cross, usually lit up. You'll find the address of all-night pharmacies (**farmácia de serviço**) displayed in all pharmacy windows.

In Portugal, pharmacies sell pharmaceutical products, and sometimes a small supply of cosmetics as well – also available in a **perfumaria**. Household items and toiletries can be bought from a **drogaria** or **mercearia**. In the pharmacies in Brazil, you can normally find medicines, perfume, cosmetics and household goods. Travelers who use prescription medicine should bring enough with them to cover their stay.

YOU MAY HEAR...

UMA VEZ/TRÊS VEZES POR DIA	once/three times a day
COMPRIMIDO(S)	tablet(s)
GOTA	drop
COLHER(ES) DE CHÁ	teaspoon(s)
ANTES DAS/DEPOIS DAS/COM AS REFEIÇÕES	before/after/with meals
COM O ESTÔMAGO VAZIO	on an empty stomach
INGIRA INTEIRO	swallow whole
PODE CAUSAR SONOLÊNCIA	may cause drowsiness
PARA USO EXTERNO	for external use only

BASIC SUPPLIES

I'd like...	**Queria...** *keh • ree • uh...*
acetaminophen [paracetamol]	**paracetamol** *puh • ruh • seh • tuh • mawl*
antiseptic cream	**uma pomada antiséptica** *oo • muh poo • mah • duh uhn • tee • sehp • tee • kuh*
aspirin	**uma aspirina** *oo • muh uhz • pee • ree • nuh*
bandages	**umas ligaduras** *oo • muhz lee • guh • doo • ruhz*
a comb	**um pente** *oong pehnt*

condoms	**uns preservativos**
	oongz preh • sehr • vuh • tee • vooz
contact lens solution	**um líquido de lente de contacto**
	oong lee • kee • thoo deh lehnt deh kaun • tahk • too
deodorant	**um desodorizante**
	oong dehz • aw • doo • ree • zuhnt
a hairbrush	**uma escova de cabelo**
	oo • muh ees • kau • vuh deh kuh • beh • loo
I'd like…	**Queria…**
	keh • ree • uh…
hair spray	**laca para o cabelo**
	lah • kuh puh • ruh oo kuh • beh • loo
ibuprofen	**ibuprofeno**
	ee • boo • praw • feh • noo
insect repellent	**um repelente para insectos**
	oong reh • peh • lehnt puh • ruh een • sehk • tooz
a nail file	**uma lima**
	oo • muh lee • muh
a (disposable) razor	**uma gilete (descartável)**
	oo • muh zsee • leht (dush • kuhr • tah • veh)
razor blades	**umas lâminas de barbear**
	oo • muhz luh • mee • nuhz deh buhr • bee • ahr
sanitary napkins [towels]	**uns pensos higiénicos**
	oongz pehn • sooz ee • zseh • nee • kooz
shampoo/ conditioner	**um shampoo/amaciador para cabelo**
	oong shuhm • poo / uh • muh • see • uh • daur puh • ruh kuh • beh • lo
soap	**um sabonete**
	oong suh • boo • neht

sunscreen	**um protector solar**
	oong praw • teh • taur soo • lahr
tampons	**uns tampões higiénicos**
	oongz tuhm • poingz ee • zseh • nee • kooz
tissues	**uns lenços de papel**
	oongz lehn • sooz deh puh • pehl
toilet paper	**papel higiénico**
	puh • pehl ee • zseh • nee • koo
toothpaste	**uma pasta de dentes**
	oo • muh pah • stuh deh dehntz

For Baby Essentials, see page 138.

CHILD HEALTH & EMERGENCY

Can you recommend a pediatrician?	**Pode recomendar um pediatra?**
	pawd reh • kau • mehn • dahr oong pee • dee • ah • truh
My child is allergic to…	**A minha criança é alérgico** m/**alérgica** f **a…**
	uh mee • nyuh kree • uhn • suh eh uh • lehr • gee • koo/uh • lehr • gee • kuh uh…
My son/daughter is missing.	**O meu filho/A minha filha desapareceu.**
	oo mehoo fee • lyoo/uh mee • nyuh fee • lyuh deh • zuh • puh • ruh • seoo
Have you seen a boy/girl?	**Viu um menino/uma menina?**
	veeoo oong meh • nee • noo/oo • muh meh • nee • nuh

For Health, see page 147.

DISABLED TRAVELERS

NEED TO KNOW

Is there...?	**Há...?**
	ah...
access for the disabled	**acesso para deficientes físicos**
	uh • seh • soo puh • ruh
	deh • fee • see • ehntz fee • see • kooz
a wheelchair ramp	**uma rampa de cadeira de rodas**
	oo • muh ruhm • puh deh kuh • day • ruh
	deh raw • thuhz
a handicapped-[disabled-] accessible toilet	**uma casa de banho acessível para deficientes**
	oo • muh kah • zuh deh buh • nyoo
	uh • seh • see • vehl puh • ruh
	deh • fee • see • ehntz
I need...	**Preciso de...**
	preh • see • zoo deh...
assistance	**assistência**
	uh • see • stehn • see • uh
an elevator [lift]	**um elevador**
	oong eh • leh • vuh • daur
a ground-floor room	**um quarto no primeiro andar**
	oong kwahr • too noo pree • may • roo
	uhn • dahr

ASKING FOR ASSISTANCE

I'm disabled.	**Sou deficiente.**
	sawoo deh • fee • see • ehnt

I'm deaf.	**Sou surdo** *m*/**Sou surda** *f*.
	sawoo <u>soor</u> • doo/sawoo <u>soor</u> • duh
I'm visually/hearing impaired.	**Vejo/Ouço mal.**
	vay • <u>zsoo</u>/ow • <u>soo</u> mahl
I'm unable to walk far/use the stairs.	**Não posso caminhar muito/usar as escadas.**
	nohm <u>paw</u> • soo kuh • mee • <u>nyahr</u> mween • tuh/oo • <u>zahr</u> uhz ee • <u>skah</u> • thuhz
Please speak louder.	**Por favor, fale mais alto.**
	poor fuh • <u>vaur fah</u> • leh mey • ez <u>ahl</u> • too
Can I bring my wheelchair?	**Posso trazer a minha cadeira de rodas?**
	<u>paw</u> • soo truh • <u>zehr</u> uh <u>mee</u> • nyuh kuh • <u>day</u> • ruh deh <u>raw</u> • duhz
Are guide dogs permitted?	**Os cães de guia são permitidos?**
	ooz kengs de <u>gee</u> • uh sohm pehr • mee • <u>tee</u> • dooz
Can you help me?	**Pode ajudar-me?**
	pawd uh • zsoo • <u>dahr</u> • meh
Please open/hold the door.	**Por favor abra/segure a porta.**
	poor fuh • <u>vaur ah</u> • bruh/seh • <u>goo</u> • reh uh <u>pawr</u> • tuh

FOOD

EATING OUT 164

MEALS
& COOKING 176

DRINKS 194

ON THE MENU 201

EATING OUT

NEED TO KNOW

Can you recommend a good restaurant/ bar?	**Pode recomendar-me um bom restaurante/bar?** *pawd reh • kaw • mehn • dahr • meh oong bohng reh • stahoo • ruhnt/bar*
Is there a(n) traditional Portuguese/ inexpensive restaurant near here?	**Há um restaurante tradicional português/barato perto daqui?** *ah oong reh • stuhoo • ruhnt truh • dee • see • oo • nahl por • too • gehz/buh • rah • too pehr • too duh • kee*
A table for…, please.	**Uma mesa para…, se faz favor.** *oo • muh meh • zuh puh • ruh…seh fahz fuh • vaur*
Could we sit…?	**Podemos sentar-nos…?** *poo • deh • mooz sehn • tahr • nooz…*
here/there	**aqui/ali** *uh • kee/uh • lee*
outside	**lá fora** *lah faw • ruh*
in a non-smoking area	**na área para não-fumadores** *nuh ah • ree • uh puh • ruh nohm foo • muh • daur • ehs*
I'm waiting for someone.	**Estou à espera de alguém.** *ee • stawoo ah ee • speh • ruh deh ahl • gehm*

Where's the restroom [toilet]?	**Onde são as casas de banho?**
	aund sohmuhz kah•zuhz deh buh•nyoo
A menu, please.	**Uma ementa, por favor.**
	oo•muh ee•mehn•tuh poor fuh•vaur
What do you recommend?	**O que é que me recomenda?**
	oo keh eh keh meh reh•koo•mehn•duh
I'd like…	**Queria…**
	keh•ree•uh…
Some more…, please.	**Mais…, se faz favor.**
	meyez…seh fahz fuh•vaur
Enjoy your meal.	**Bom apetite.**
	bohng uh•peh•tee•teh
The check [bill], please.	**A conta, por favor.**
	uh kaum•tuh poor fuh•vaur
Is service included?	**O serviço está incluído?**
	oo sehr•vee•soo ee•stah een•kloo•ee•thoo
Can I pay by credit card?	**Posso pagar com cartão de crédito?**
	paw•soo puh•gahr kaum kuhr•tohm deh kreh•dee•too
Could I have a receipt, please?	**Pode darme uma factura, por favor?**
	pawd dahr•meh oo•muh fah•too•ruh poor fuh•vaur
Thank you.	**Obrigado** m/**Obrigada** f.
	aw•bree•gah•thoo/ aw•bree•gah•thuh

WHERE TO EAT

Can you recommend…?	**Pode recomendar-me…?**
	pawd reh • koo • mehn • dahr • meh…
a restaurant	**um restaurante**
	oong reh • stuhoo • ruhnt
a bar	**um bar**
	oong bar
a cafe	**um café**
	oong kuh • feh
a fast-food place	**um restaurante de comida rápida**
	oong reh • stuhoo • ruhnt deh koo • mee • duh rah • pee • duh
a seafood restaurant	**uma marisqueira**
	oo • muh muh • ree • skay • ruh
a cheap restaurant	**um restaurante barato**
	oong rehz • tahoo • ruhnt buh • rah • too
an expensive resturant	**um restaurante caro**
	oong rehz • tahoo • ruhnt kah • roo
a restaurant with a good view	**um restaurante com boa vista**
	oong rehz • tahoo • ruhnt kaum bau • uh vee • stuh

| an authentic/ non-touristy restaurant | **um restaurante típico/não turístico** |
| | *oong rehz • tahoo • ruhnt tee • pee • koo/ nohm too • ree • stee • koo* |

For On the Menu, see page 201.

RESERVATIONS & PREFERENCES

I'd like to reserve a table…	**Queria reservar uma mesa…**
	keh • <u>ree</u> • uh reh • zehr • <u>vahr</u> <u>oo</u> • muh <u>meh</u> • zuh…
for two	**para dois**
	<u>puh</u> • ruh doyz
for this evening	**para hoje à noite**
	<u>puh</u> • ruh auzseh ah noyt
for tomorrow at…	**para amanhã às…**
	<u>puh</u> • ruh uh • muh • <u>nyuh</u> ahz…
A table for two.	**Uma mesa para dois.**
	<u>oo</u> • muh <u>meh</u> • zuh <u>puh</u> • ruh doyz
We have a reservation.	**Temos uma reserva.**
	<u>teh</u> • mooz <u>oo</u> • muh reh • <u>zehr</u> • vuh
My name is…	**Chamo-me…**
	<u>shuh</u> • moo • meh…
Could we sit…?	**Podemos sentar-nos…?**
	poo • <u>deh</u> • mooz sehn • <u>tahr</u> • nooz…
here/there	**aqui/ali**
	uh • <u>kee</u>/uh • <u>lee</u>
outside	**lá fora**
	lah <u>faw</u> • ruh
in a non-smoking area	**na área para não-fumadores**
	nuh <u>ah</u> • ree • uh <u>puh</u> • ruh nohm foo • muh • <u>daur</u> • ehs
by the window	**à janela**
	ah zsuh • <u>neh</u> • luh

in the shade	**à sombra**
	ah sohng • bruh
in the sun	**ao sol**
	ahoo sawl
Where are the restrooms [toilets]?	**Onde são as casas de banho?**
	aund sohmuhz <u>kah</u> • zuhz deh <u>buh</u> • nyoo

YOU MAY HEAR...

Tem reserva?	Do you have a reservation?
teng reh • <u>sehr</u> • vuh	
Quantas pessoas?	How many?
<u>kwuhn</u> • tuhz peh • <u>sau</u> • uhs	
Fumador ou não-fumador?	Smoking or non-smoking?
foo • muh • <u>daur</u> aw	
*noh**m**foo • muh • <u>daur</u>*	
Deseja encomendar?	Would you like to order?
deh • <u>zeh</u> • zsuh	
ehn • caw • mehn • <u>dahr</u>	
O que deseja?	What would you like?
oo keh deh • <u>zeh</u> • zsuh	
Recomendo...	I recommend...
reh • koo • <u>mehn</u> • doo...	
Bom apetite.	Enjoy your meal.
bohng uh • peh • <u>tee</u> • teh	

HOW TO ORDER

Excuse me!	**Se faz favor!**
	seh fahz fuh • <u>vaur</u>
We're ready to order.	**Estamos prontos para encomendar.**
	ee • <u>stuh</u> • mooz <u>prawn</u> • tooz puh • ruh
	eng • kau • mehn • <u>dahr</u>

The wine list, please.	**A carta dos vinhos, se faz favor.**
	uh kahr • tuh dooz vee • nyooz seh fahz fuh • vaur
I'd like…	**Queria…**
	keh • ree • uh…
a bottle of…	**uma garrafa…**
	oo • muh guh • rrah • fuh…
a carafe of…	**um jarro de…**
	oomjah • rroo deh…
a glass of…	**um copo de…**
	oong kaw • poo deh…
A menu, please.	**Uma ementa, por favor.**
	oo • muh ee • mehn • tuh poor fuh • vaur
Do you have…?	**Tem…?**
	teng…
a menu in English	**uma ementa em Inglês**
	oo • muh ee • mehn • tuh eng een • glehz
a fixed-price menu	**uma ementa de preço-fixo**
	oo • muh ee • mehn • tuh deh preh • soo feek • soo
a children's menu	**uma ementa de criança**
	oo • muh ee • mehn • tuh deh kree • uhn • suh
What do you recommend?	**O que é que me recomenda?**
	oo kee eh keh meh reh • koo • mehn • duh
What's this?	**O que é isto?**
	oo kee eh ee • stoo
What's in it?	**Leva o quê?**
	leh • vuh oo keh
Is it spicy?	**É picante?**
	eh pee • kuhnt
I'd like…	**Queria…**
	keh • ree • uh…

More…, please.	**Mais…, se faz favor.**
	meyez…seh fahz fuh • vaur
With/Without…	**Com/Sem…**
	kaum/seng…
I can't have…	**Não posso ter…**
	nohmpaw • soo tehr…
rare	**mal passado** *m*/**passada** *f*
	mahl puh • sah • thoo/
	puh • sah • thuh
medium	**meio passado** *m*/**passada** *f*
	may • oo puh • sah • thoo/
	puh • sah • thuh
well-done	**bem passado** *m*/**passada** *f*
	beng puh • sah • thoo/
	puh • sah • thuh
It's to go.	**É para levar.**
[take away]	*eh puh • ruh leh • vahr*

YOU MAY SEE…

COUVERT	cover charge
PREÇO-FIXO	fixed-price
EMENTA	menu
UMA EMENTA DO DIA	menu of the day
SERVIÇO (NÃO) INCLUÍDO	service (not) included
ESPECIAIS	specials

COOKING METHODS

baked	**alourado** m/**alourada** f
	uh • lauoo • _rah_ • thoo/
	uh • lauoo • _rah_ • thuh
boiled	**cozido** m/**cozida** f
	koo • _zee_ • thoo/koo • _zee_ • thuh
braised	**estufado** m/**estufada** f
	ee • stoo • _fah_ • thoo/
	ee • stoo • _fah_ • thuh
breaded	**panado** m/**panada** f
	puh • _nah_ • thoo/puh • _nah_ • thuh
creamed	**com natas**
	kohng _nah_ • tuhz
diced	**aos cubos**
	ahooz _koo_ • booz
filet of…	**filete de…**
	fee • _leht_ deh…
fried	**frito** m/**frita** f
	f _free_ • too/_free_ • tuh
grilled	**grelhado** m/**grelhada** f
	gree • _lyah_ • thoo/gree • _lyah_ • thuh
poached	**escalfado** m/**escalfada** f
	ees • kahl • _fah_ • thoo/
	ees • kahl • _fah_ • thuh
roasted	**assado** m/**assada** f
	uh • _sah_ • thoo/uh • _sah_ • thuh
sautéed	**salteado** m/**salteada** f
	sahl • tee • _ah_ • thoo/
	sahl • tee • _ah_ • thuh
smoked	**fumado** m/**fumada** f
	foo • _mah_ • thoo/foo • _mah_ • thuh

steamed	**cozido** m/**cozida** f **a vapor**
	koo • <u>zee</u> • thoo/koo • <u>zee</u> • thuh uh
	vuh • <u>paur</u>
stewed	**guisado** m/**guisada** f
	gee • <u>zah</u> • thoo/gee • <u>zah</u> • thuh
stuffed	**recheado** m/**recheada** f
	reh • shee • <u>ah</u> • thoo/reh • shee • <u>ah</u> • thuh

DIETARY REQUIREMENTS

I am…	**Sou…**
	sauoo…
diabetic	**diabético** m/**diabética** f
	dee • uh • <u>beh</u> • tee • koo/
	dee • uh • <u>beh</u> • tee • kuh
lactose intolerant	**intolerante à lactose**
	een • tawl • eh • <u>ruhnt</u> ah <u>lahk</u> • tawz
vegetarian	**vegetariano** m/**vegetariana** f
	veh • zseh • tuh • ree • <u>uh</u> • noo/
	veh • zseh • tuh • ree • <u>uh</u> • nuh
vegan	**vegetariano**
	veh • geh • tuh • ree • uh • noo
I'm allergic to…	**Sou alérgico** m/**alérgica** f **a…**
	sauoo uh • <u>lehr</u> • gee • koo/
	uh • <u>lehr</u> • gee • kuh uh…
I can't eat…	**Não posso comer…**
	nohm <u>paw</u> • soo koo • <u>mehr</u>…
dairy	**lacticínios**
	lahk • tee • <u>see</u> • nee • ooz
gluten	**glúten**
	gloo • <u>tehn</u>
nuts	**nozes**
	<u>naw</u> • zehz
pork	**carne de porco**
	<u>kahrr</u> • neh deh <u>paur</u> • koo

shellfish	**marisco**
	muh • _ree_ • skoo
spicy foods	**comidas picantes**
	koo • _mee_ • duhz pee • _kuhnts_
wheat	**trigo**
	tree • goo
Is it halal/kosher?	**É halal/kosher?**
	eh uh • _lahl_/_kaw_ • shehr
Do you have...?	**Tem...?**
	teng...
skimmed milk	**leite magro**
	layt mah • groo
whole milk	**leite gordo**
	layt goahr • doo
soya milk	**leite de soja**
	layt deh saw • zsuh

DINING WITH CHILDREN

Do you have children's portions?	**Tem doses para crianças?**
	teng _daw_ • zehs _puh_ • ruh kree • _uhn_ • suhz
A child's seat, please.	**Um assento de criança, por favor.**
	oong uh • _sehn_ • too deh kree • _uhn_ • suh poor fuh • _vaur_
Can I have a highchair/child's seat?	**Tem uma cadeira alta/ cadeirinha de criança?**
	teng oo • muh kuh • day • ruh ahl • tuh/ kuh • day • ree • nyuh deh kree • uhn • suh
Where can I feed/ change the baby?	**Onde posso alimentar/mudar o bebé?**
	aund _paw_ • soo uh • lee • mehn • _tahr_/ moo • _dahr_ oo beh • beh
Can you warm this?	**Pode aquecer isto?**
	pawd uh • keh • _sehr ee_ • stoo

For Traveling with Children, see page 136.

HOW TO COMPLAIN

How much longer will our food be?	**Quanto tempo demora a nossa comida?** *kwuhn • too tehm • poo deh • maw • ruh uh naw • suh koo • mee • thuh*
We can't wait any longer.	**Não podemos esperar mais.** *nohm poo • deh • mooz ee • speh • rahr meyez*
We're leaving.	**Vamo-nos embora.** *vuh • moo • nooz ehm • baw • ruh*
I didn't order this.	**Não encomendei isso.** *nohm ehn • koo • mehn • day ee • soo*
I ordered…	**Encomendei…** *ehn • koo • mehn • day…*
I can't eat this.	**Não posso comer isto.** *nohm paw • soo koo • mehr ee • stoo*
This is too…	**Isto está muito…** *ee • stoo ee • stah mooee • too…*
cold/hot	**frio/quente** *free • oo/kehnt*
salty/spicy	**salgado/picante** *sahl • gah • thoo/pee • kuhnt*
tough/bland	**duro/insosso** *doo • roo/een • saw • soo*

This isn't clean/ fresh.	**Isto não está limpo/fresco.**
	ee • stoo nohm ee • <u>stah</u> <u>leem</u> • poo/ <u>frehs</u> • koo

PAYING

The check [bill], please.	**A conta, por favor.**
	uh <u>kaum</u> • tuh poor fuh • <u>vaur</u>
Separate checks [bills], please.	**Contas separadas, por favor.**
	<u>kaum</u> • tuhz seh • puh • <u>rah</u> • duhz poor fuh • <u>vaur</u>
It's all together.	**É tudo junto.**
	eh <u>too</u> • doo <u>zsoon</u> • too
Is service included?	**O serviço está incluído?**
	oo sehr • <u>vee</u> • soo ee • <u>stah</u> een • kloo • <u>ee</u> • thoo
What's this amount for?	**De que é este valor?**
	deh keh eh <u>eh</u> • stuh vuh • <u>loahr</u>
I didn't have that. I had…	**Eu não comi isso. Eu comi…**
	ehoo nohm koo • <u>mee</u> <u>ee</u> • soo. ehoo koo • <u>mee</u>…
Can I pay by credit card?	**Posso pagar com cartão de crédito?**
	<u>paw</u> • soo puh • <u>gahr</u> kaum kuhr • <u>tohm</u> deh <u>kreh</u> • dee • too
Can I have an itemized bill/ a receipt?	**Pode dar-me uma conta detalhada/uma factura?**
	pawd <u>dahr</u> • meh oo • muh <u>kaum</u> • tuh deh • tuh • <u>lyah</u> • duh/<u>oo</u> • muh fah • <u>too</u> • ruh
That was a very good meal.	**Foi uma refeição excelente.**
	foy <u>oo</u> • muh reh • fay • <u>sohm</u> eh • seh • <u>lehnt</u>
I've already paid.	**Já paguei.**
	zsah puh • gay.

ⓘ

Portuguese food is largely inspired by its location off
the Atlantic Ocean; much of its cuisine is comprised of fish,
especially salted cod. Typical Portuguese food is often the
simple, delicious fare of fisherman and farmers. Expect to
find fish, meat, rice and potatoes combined with olive oil
and wine. Restaurant owners and wait staff are generally
extremely friendly.

MEALS & COOKING

BREAKFAST

a água	water
uh <u>ah</u> • gwuh	
o bolinho	muffin
oo bau • <u>lee</u> • nyoo	
o café.../chá...	coffee.../tea...
oo kuh • <u>feh</u>.../shah...	
com açúcar	with sugar
kaum uh • <u>soo</u> • kuhr	
com adoçante artificial	with artificial
kaum uh • thoo • <u>suhnt</u>	sweetner
uhr • tee • fee • see • <u>ahl</u>	
com leite	with milk
kaum layt	
descafeínado	decaf
dehz • kuh • fay • <u>nah</u> • thoo	
bica	black
<u>bee</u> • kuh	

O pequeno almoço
Breakfast (known as **café da manhã** in Brazil) is usually served from 7:00 to 10:00 a.m. In Portugal it is comprised of coffee, rolls, butter and jam and sometimes fruit juice, fruit, toast and pastry makes for a heartier meal.

O almoço
Lunch is the main meal of the day, served from12:30 to 2:30 p.m. Shops are normally closed during these hours. It generally includes soup or salad, fish or meat, and a dessert.

O jantar
Dinner is served fromabout 7:30 to 10:00 p.m., except in a Portuguese **casa de fado** ('house of blues' dinner theater), where dinner is served a bit later. It typically includes soup, fish or meat, salad, bread, and fruit or a sweet for dessert. Coffee or espresso is almost always served at the end of every meal.

as carnes frias	cold cuts
uhz kahr • nehz free • uhz	[charcuterie]
o cereal (frio/quente)	(cold/hot) cereal
oo seh • ree • ahl (free • oo/kehnt)	
o doce de fruta	jam
oo dau • seh deh froo • tuh	
a farinha de aveia	oatmeal
uh fuh • ree • nyuh deh uh • vay • uh	
o leite	milk
oo layt	
a manteiga	butter
uh muhn • tay • guh	

a omelete omelet
uh aw • meh • leh • tuh

o iogurte yogurt
uh yaw • goort

o ovo... ...egg
oo au • voo...

  muito fervido/fervido macio hard-boiled/soft-boiled
  *mooee • too fehr • vee • thoo/
  fehr • vee • thoo muh • see • oo*

  estrelado fried
  ee • struh • lah • doo

  mexido scrambled
  meh • shee • doo

o pão bread
oo pohm

o papo-seco roll
*oo pah • poo
seh • koo*

o queijo cheese
oo kay • zsoo

as salsichas sausages
uhz sahl • see • shuhz

o sumo de... ...juice
oo soo • moo deh

  fruta fruit
  froo • tuh

  maçã apple
  muh • suh

  toranja grapefruit
  uh taw • ruhn • zsuh

  laranja orange
  luh • ruhn • zsuh

o toucinho bacon
oo taw • see • nyoo

as torradas	toast
uhz too • rrah • duhz	
o yogurte	yogurt
oo yaw • goort	

APPETIZERS

as carnes frias	cold cuts
uhz kahr • nehz free • uhz	
o chouriço	sausage
oo shauoo • ree • soo	
as lulas à milanesa	squid
uhz loo • luhz ah mee • luh • neh • zuh	
o paio	smoked pork fillet
oo peye • oo	
os pimentos assados	roasted peppers
ooz pee • mehn • tooz uh • sah • dooz	
o pipis	spicy chicken stew
oo pee • peez	
a santola recheada	stuffed crab
uh suhn • taw • luh eh • shee • ah • thuh	

SOUP

o caldo verde	potato and kale soup with sausage
oo kahl • doo vehrd	
o gaspacho	chilled soup with tomatoes, sweet peppers, onions, cucumbers and croutons
oo guhz • pah • shoo	
as migas de bacalhau	dried cod soup with garlic and bread
uhz mee • guhz deh buh • kuh • lyahoo	

a sopa açorda à Alentejana
a sau • puh uh • saur • duh ah
uh • luhn • teh • zsuh • nuh
bread soup with garlic and herbs

a sopa de cozido
a sau • puh deh koo • zee • doo
meat broth with vegetables and macaroni

a sopa seca
uh sau • puh seh • kuh
thick soup with meat, cabbage and bread

a sopa transmontana
a sau • puh truhnz • moo • tuh • nuh
vegetable soup with bacon and bread

a sopa...
uh sau • puh...
...soup

à pescador
ah pehs • kuh • daur
fish

canja
keng • zsuh
chicken and rice

de abóbora
deh uh • baw • buh • ruh
pumpkin

de agriões
deh uh • gree • oings
potato and watercress

de coentros
deh koo • eng • trooz
coriander, bread, and poached eggs

de ervilhas
deh eer • vee • lyuhz
green pea

Salt cod or **bacalhau** is hugely popular - try the bolinhos de bacalhau (cod fish balls) as an appetizer or **bacalhau dourado** or **bacalhau à brás** (two similar dishes of cod with scrambled eggs, onions and shoestring potatoes). **Bacalhau à Gomes de Sá** is another famous dish.

FISH & SEAFOOD

o atum	tuna
oo uh • toong	
as amêijoas à Bulhão Pato	clams with coriander,
uhz uh • may • zsoo • uhz ah boo • lyohm	garlic and onion
pah • too	
as amêijoas à Portuguesa	clams with garlic,
uhz uh • may • zsoo • uhz ah	parsley and olive oil
poor • too • geh • zuh	olive oil
o bacalhau à Gomes de Sá	casserole of dried
oo buh • kuh • lyahoo ah gau • mehz	cod with olives,
deh sah	garlic, onions,
	parsley and hard-
	boiled eggs
o bacalhau podre	baked layers of cod
oo buh • kuh • lyahoo pau • dreh	and fried potatoes
a cabeça de pescada cozida	fish stew
uh kuh • beh • suh deh peh • skah • thuh	
koo • zee • thuh	
os camarões…	…shrimp [prawns]
ooz kuh • muh • roings…	
fritos	fried
free • tooz	
grandes	large [king]
gruhn • dehz	
no espeto	on a stick
noo ee • speh • too	
a caldeirada…	fish with onions,
uh kahl • day • rah • thuh…	tomatoes, potatoes,
	olive oil…

à fragateira
ah fruh • guh • tay • ruh

shellfish and mussels in a fish stock with tomatoes

à moda da Póvoa
ah maw • duh duh praw • voo • uh

hake, skate, sea bass and eel

o espadarte
oo ees • puh • dahrt

swordfish

a lagosta
uh luh • gau • stuh

lobster

a lampreia
uh luhm • pray • uh

lamprey

o linguado
oo leeng • gwah • thoo

sole

as lulas
uhz loo • luhz

squid

as lulas recheadas
uhz loo • luhz reh • shee • ah • duhz

stuffed squid

os mariscos
ooz muh • rees • kooz

seafood

as ostras do Algarve
uhz aw • struhz thoo ahl • gahrv

oysters in butter and wine (Algarve)

o pargo
oo pahr • goo

bream

o polvo
oo paul • voo

octopus

o vatapá
oo vuh • tuh • pah

fish and shrimp in a paste made of flour

MEAT & POULTRY

o arroz de frango
oo uh • rrauz deh fruhn • goo
chicken with white wine, hamand rice

o bife
oo beef
steak

o bife na frigideira
oo beef nuh free • zsuh • day • ruh
steak fried in butter, white wine and garlic

o borrego
oo boo • rreh • goo
lamb

a carne de porco
uh kahrn deh paur • koo
pork

a carne de vaca
uh kahrn deh vah • kuh
beef

o carneiro guisado
oo kuhrr • nay • roo gee • zah • thoo
mutton with tomatoes, garlic and herbs

o coelho
oo koo • eh • lyoo
rabbit

a costeleta
uh koo • stuh • leh • tuh
cutlet

o cozido à Portuguesa
oo koo • zee • doo ah poor • too • geh • zuh
boiled beef, bacon, smoked sausage and vegetables

a feijoada
uh fay • zsoo • ah • duh
Brazil's national dish: black beans cooked with bacon, salted pork, jerky and sausage

o frango
oo fruhn • goo
chicken

o frango na púcara
oo fruhn • goo nuh poo • keh • ruh

chicken stewed in port and cognac, then fried with almonds

o medalhão
uh meh • duh • lyohm

tenderloin steak

a perdiz à caçador
oo pehr • deez uh kuh • suh • daur

partridge simmered with carrots, onions, white wine and herbs

o presunto
oo preh • zoon • too

cured ham

as tripas à moda do Porto
uhz tree • puhz ah maw • duh thoo paur • too

tripe cooked with pork, beans and chicken

a vitela
uh vee • tehl • uh

veal

o xinxim de galinha
oo sheeng • sheeng deh guh • lee • nyuh

chicken cooked in dried shrimp, peanuts and parsley

In Portugal, many dishes are served with both rice and potatoes. Almost every meal is served with a salad. Portugal is not a very vegetarian-friendly country, and vegetarians may have a difficult time finding meals in restaurants outside of Lisbon, Porto or the Algarve.

VEGETABLES & STAPLES

o açafrão
oo uh • suh • frohm   saffron

o açúcar
oo uh • soo • kuhr   sugar

as alcaparras
uhz ahl • kuh • pah • rruhz   capers

a alface
uh ahl • fah • seh   lettuce

as amêndoas
uhz uh • mehn • doo • uhz   almonds

o arroz...
oo uh • rrauz...   rice...

  de alhos
  deh ah • lyooz   with garlic

  de cozido
  deh koo • zee • thoo   cooked in meat stock

  de feijão
  de fay • zsohm   with beans

as batatas...
uhz buh • tah • tuhz...   potatoes...

  cozidas
  koo • zee • duhz   boiled

  cozidas com pele
  koo • zee • duhz kohm pehl boiled in their skins

  fritas
  free • tuhz   fries [chips]

  de palha
  deh pah • lyuh   matchsticks

o puré de batatas
oo poo • reh deh buh • tah • tuhz   mashed potatoes

as cebolas
uhz seh • bau • luhz   onions

os cogumelos *ooz koo • goo • <u>meh</u> • looz*	mushrooms
as ervilhas *uhz eer • <u>vee</u> • lyuhz*	peas
a farinha *uh fuh • <u>ree</u> • nyuh*	flour
as favas *uhz <u>fah</u> • vuhz*	broad beans
o feijão *oo fay • <u>zsohm</u>*	kidney beans
o feijão verde *oo fay • <u>zsohm</u> vehrd*	green beans
o manjericão *oo muhn • zseh • ree • <u>kohm</u>*	basil
a manteiga *uh muhn • <u>tay</u> • guh*	butter
as massas *uhz <u>mah</u> • suhz*	pasta
o pão *oo pohm*	bread
os pimentos *ooz pee • <u>mehn</u> • tooz*	peppers
a salsa *uh <u>sahl</u> • suh*	parsley

FRUIT

o abacate oo uh • buh • _kaht_	avocado
o abacaxi oo uh • buh • _kah_ • shee	pineapple
os alperces ooz uhl • _pehr_ • sehz	apricots
as ameixas uhz uh • _may_ • shuhz	plums
o arando oo uh • _ruhn_ • doo	cranberry
a banana uh buh • _nuh_ • nuh	banana
as cerejas uhz seh • _ray_ • zsuhz	cherries
o coco oo _kaw_ • koo	coconut
a framboesa uh fruhm • _booeh_ • zuh	raspberry
a fruta uh _froo_ • tuh	fruit
a goiaba uh goy • _ah_ • buh	guava
o kiwi oo kee • _wee_	kiwi
a laranja uh luh • _ruhn_ • zsuh	orange
a lima uh _lee_ • muh	lime
o limão oo lee • _mohm_	lemon
a maçã uh muh • _suh_	apple

o mamão *oo muh • mohm*	papaya
a manga *uh muhn • guh*	mango
a mexerica *uh meh • sheh • ree • kuh*	tangerine
a melancia *uh muh • luhn • see • uh*	watermelon
o melão *oo meh • lohm*	melon
o mirtilo *oo meer • tee • loo*	blueberry
os morangos *ooz moo • ruhn • gooz*	strawberries
a pêra *uh peh • ruh*	pear
o pêssego *oo pay • seh • goo*	peach
a toranja *uh taw • ruhn • zsa*	grapefruit
as uvas *uhz oo • vuhz*	grapes

CHEESE

o azeitão *oo uh • zay • tohm*	creamy cheese
a bola *uh bau • luh*	hard cow's milk cheese
o cabreiro *oo kuh • bray • roo*	goat's milk cheese
o castelo branco *oo kuh • steh • loo bruhn • koo*	creamy blue cheese
a évora *uh eh • voo • ruh*	creamy cheese

a ilha
uh ee • lyuh

cow's milk cheese
from the Azores
Islands

o queijo
oo kay • zsoo

cheese

o queijo de Minas
oo • kay • zsoo deh mee • nuhz

Brazilian cow's milk
cheese

o requeijão
oo reh • kay • zsohm

creamy Brazilian
cheese

o serra
oo she • rruh

creamy goat's milk
cheese

macio
muh • see • oo

soft

duro
doo • roo

hard

suave
swahv

mild

forte
fawrt

strong

DESSERT

a arrufada de Coimbra
uh uh • rroo • fah • duh deh kooeem • bruh

cinnamon dough
cake

a babá-de-moça
uh buh • bah deh mau • suh

dessert made of egg
yolk, coconut milk
and syrup (Braz.)

o bolo podre
oo bau • loo pau • dreh

honey and cinnamon
cake

as broas castelares
uhz brau • uhz kuh • steh • lah • rehz

sweet-potato
biscuits

a canjica
uh kuhn • zsee • kuh

dessert made with
sweet corn and milk
(Braz.)

a goiabada
uh goy • uh • <u>bah</u> • duh

thick paste made of guavas (Braz.)

a mousse de maracujá
*uh <u>moo</u> • seh deh
muh • ruh • koo • <u>zsah</u>*

passion fruit mousse (Braz.)

os ovos moles de Aveiro
ooz <u>aw</u> • vooz mawlz deh ah • <u>vay</u> • roo

egg yolks cooked in syrup

o pastel de Tentúgal
oo puhz • <u>tehl</u> deh tehn • <u>too</u> • gahl

pastry filled with egg yolks cooked in syrup

pudim flan
poo • <u>deeng</u> fluhn

caramel custard

pasteis de Belém
puhz • <u>tehz</u> de bel • ehm

small custard tartlets, famous in Lisbon

SAUCES & CONDIMENTS

o sal
o sahl

salt

a pimenta
uh pee • <u>mehn</u> • tuh

pepper

mostarda
mooz • tahr • duh

mustard

ketchup
ketchup

ketchup

AT THE MARKET

Where are the trolleys/ baskets?	**Onde estão os carrinhos/cestos?** *aund ee • <u>stohm</u> ooz kuh • <u>rree</u> • nyooz/<u>sehs</u> • tooz*
Where is…?	**Onde é…?** *aund eh…*

YOU MAY HEAR...

Deseja alguma coisa?
deh • zeh • zsuh ahl • goo • muh coy • zuh

Would you like something?

O que é que deseja?
oo kee eh keh deh • zeh • zsuh

What would you like?

Mais alguma coisa?
meyez ahl • goo • muh coy • zuh

Anything else?

São...euros.
sohm...ehoo • rooz

That's...euros.

I'd like some of that/those.	**Queria disso/desses.** *keh • ree • uh thee • soo/theh • sehz*
Can I taste it?	**Posso provar?** *paw • soo proo • vahr*
I'd like...	**Queria...** *keh • ree • uh...*
a kilo/half-kilo of...	**um quilo/meio quilo de...** *oong kee • loo/may • oo kee • loo deh...*
a liter/half-liter of...	**um litro/meio litro de...** *oong lee • troo/may • oo lee • troo deh...*
I'd like...	**Queria...** *keh • ree • uh...*
a piece of...	**uma fatia de...** *oo • muh fuh • tee • uh deh...*
a slice of...	**um pedaço de...** *oong peh • dah • soo deh...*
More./Less.	**Mais./Menos.** *meyez/meh • nooz*
How much?	**Quanto é?** *kwuhn • too eh*
Where do I pay?	**Onde pago?** *aund pah • goo*

A bag, please.	**Un saco, por favor.**
	oong sah • koo poor fuh • vaur
I'm being helped.	**Alguém está a ajudar-me.**
	ahl • geng ee • stah uh
	uh • zsoo • dahr • meh

ℹ️

Street markets are an integral part of Portuguese life, but you must get there early to get the full experience. By 10:00 a.m. the best things are gone. Most markets are held in the town square on a weekly basis. Everything can be found here, from quality food, antiques and handicrafts to household items and clothes. Larger towns and cities may have covered markets that are open Monday through Saturday where you can buy fresh fish, meat, fruit and vegetables. Portuguese cheese, both delicious and inexpensive, is one of the most popular items at any market.

IN THE KITCHEN

bottle opener	**o abre-garrafas**
	oo ah • breh guh • rrah • fuhz
bowl	**a malga**
	uh mahl • guh
can opener	**o abre-latas**
	oo ah • breh lah • tuhz
corkscrew	**o saca-rolhas**
	oo sah • kuh rau • lyuhz
cups	**as chávenas**
	uhz shah • vee • nuhz
forks	**os garfos**
	ooz gahr • fooz

frying pan	**a frigideira**	
	uh free • zsee • thay • ruh	
glasses	**os copos**	
	ooz kaw • pooz	
knife	**as facas**	
	uhz fah • kuhz	
measuring cup/	**o copo/a colher de medir**	
spoon	*oo kaw • poo/uh koo • lyehr deh meh • deer*	
paper napkin	**o guardanapo de papel**	
	oo gwahr • duh • nah • poo deh puh • pehl	
plates	**os pratos**	
	ooz prah • tooz	
pot	**a panela**	
	uh puh • neh • luh	
saucepan	**o tacho**	
	oo tah • shoo	
spatula	**a espátula**	
	uh ees • pah • too • luh	
spoon	**as colheres**	
	uhz koo • lyeh • rehz	

YOU MAY SEE...

USAR ATÉ...	best if used by...
CALORIAS	calories
SEM GORDURA	fat free
MANTER NO FRIO	keep refrigerated
PODE CONTER VESTÍGIOS DE...	may contain traces of...
MICROONDAS	microwaveable
DATA DE VENDA...	sell by...
PRÓPRIO PARA VEGETARIANOS	suitable for vegetarians

DRINKS

NEED TO KNOW

The wine list/drink menu, please.
A carta dos vinhos/ementa de bebidas, se faz favor.
uh kahr • tuh dooz vee • nyooz/ ee • mehn • tuh deh beh • bee • duhz seh fahz fuh • vaur

What do you recommend?
O que é que me recomenda?
oo keh eh keh meh reh • koo • mehn • duh

I'd like a bottle/ glass of red/white wine.
Queria uma garrafa/um copo de vinho tinto/branco.
keh • ree • uh oo • muh guh • rrah • fuh/ oong kaw • poo deh vee • nyoo teen • too/ bruhn • koo

The house wine, please.
O vinho da casa, se faz favor.
oo vee • nyoo duh kah • zuh seh fahz fuh • vaur

Another bottle/ glass, please.
Outra garrafa/Outro copo, se faz favor.
auoo • truh guh • rrah • fuh/auoo • troo kaw • poo ser fahz fuh • vaur

I'd like a local beer.
Gostaria uma cerveja local.
goo • stuh • ree • uh oo • muh sehr • vay • zsuh loo • kahl

Can I buy you a drink?
Posso oferecer-lhe uma bebida?
paw • soo aw • freh • sehr • lyeh oo • muh beh • bee • thuh

Cheers!
Viva!
vee • vuh

A coffee/tea, please.	**Um café/chá, se faz favor.**
	oong kuh • <u>feh</u>/shah seh fahz fuh • <u>vaur</u>
Black.	**Bica.**
	<u>bee</u> • kuh
With…	**com…**
	kaum…
milk	**leite**
	layt
sugar	**açúcar**
	uh • <u>soo</u> • kuhr
artificial sweetener	**adoçante**
	uh • doo • <u>suhnty</u>
A…, please.	**…, se faz favor.**
	…seh fahz fuh • <u>vaur</u>
juice	**Um sumo**
	oong <u>soo</u> • moo
soda	**Um refresco**
	oong reh • <u>freh</u> • skoo
sparkling/still water	**Uma água com/sem gás**
	<u>oo</u>-muh <u>ah</u> • gwuh kaum/sehmgahz
Is the tap water safe to drink?	**A água da torneira é boa para beber?**
	uh <u>ah</u> • gwuh duh toor • <u>nay</u> • ruh eh <u>baw</u> • uh <u>puh</u> • ruh beh • <u>behr</u>

NON-ALCOHOLIC DRINKS

a água de coco
uh ah • gwuh deh kau • koo

coconut juice

a água com/sem gás
uh ah • gwuh kaum/
sehn gahz

carbonated/
noncarbonated
[still] water

o chá frio
oo shah free • oo

iced tea

o café
oo kuh • feh

coffee

o caldo de cana
oo kahl • doo deh kuh • nuh

sugar-cane juice

o leite
oo layt

milk

o leite de coco
oo layt deh kau • koo

coconut milk

o sumo
oo soo • moo

juice

o refresco
oo reh • fray • skoo

soda

Keep an eye out for the bars advertising **sumo** (juice)
with lots of fresh fruit on display – they're a great stop for a
refreshing drink.
Sumol® is the oldest brand name of fruit juice and is found
in almost every shop selling food. It is a lightly carbonated
orange drink.

YOU MAY HEAR...

Posso oferecer-lhe uma bebida?
paw • soo aw • freh • <u>sehr</u> • lyeh <u>oo</u> • muh beh • <u>bee</u> • thuh

Can I get you a drink?

Com leite/açúcar?
kaumlayt/uh • <u>soo</u> • kuhr

With milk/sugar?

Água com ou sem gás?
<u>ah</u> • gwuh kaum auoo seng gahz

Carbonated or non-carbonated [still] water?

APERITIFS, COCKTAILS & LIQUEURS

guardente de...
h • gwahr • <u>thent</u> deh...

tequila with...

    figo
    <u>fee</u> • goo

fig

    medronho
    meh • <u>draw</u> • nyoo

arbutus berry (a small strawberry-like fruit)

    velha
    <u>veh</u> • lyuh

brandy

batida...
h buh • <u>tee</u> • duh...

cane spirit with fruit juice, sugar, ice and...

    de cajú
    deh kuh • <u>zsoo</u>

cashew nut

    de coco
    deh <u>kau</u> • koo

coconut

    de maracujá
    deh muh • ruh • koo • <u>zsah</u>

passion fruit

a caipirinha *uh keye • pee • <u>ree</u> • nyuh*	cane spirit, crushed lime, sugar and ice, originating in Brazil
a Cuba livre *uh <u>koo</u> • buh lee • vreh*	rum and Coke®
a genebra *uh zseh • <u>neh</u> • bruh*	gin
a ginjinha *uh zseeng • <u>zsee</u> • nyuh*	spirit distilled from morello cherries
o uísque *oo <u>wees</u> • keh*	whiskey
o vermute *oo vehr • <u>moot</u>*	vermouth
a tequila *uh teh • <u>kee</u> • luh*	tequila
o rum *oo roong*	rum
a vodca *uh <u>vaw</u> • dee • kuh*	vodka

BEER

a cerveja *uh sehr • <u>vay</u> • zsuh*	beer
a cerveja branca *uh sehr • <u>vay</u> • zsuh <u>bruhn</u> • kuh*	lager
a cerveja preta *uh sehr • <u>vay</u> • zsuh <u>preh</u> • tuh*	dark beer
cerveja leve *sehr • veh • zsuh leh • veh*	light beer
a imperial *uh eem • <u>peh</u> • ree • ahl*	draft [draught] beer
engarrafada *ehn • guh • rruh • fah • duh*	bottled

ocal/importada   local imported
oo • kahl/eem • pawr • tah • duh

sem álcool   non-alcoholic
seng ahl • kawl

Beer is a popular drink in Portugal. Try out some of
the local brews, such as **Sagres** or **Super Bock**. In Portugal,
beer is often served with **tremoços** (salted lupini beans) or
amendoins (peanuts).

WINE

o vinho…   …wine
oo vee • nyoo…

  de casa/mesa   house/table
  deh kah • zuh/meh • zuh

  (da) Madeira   (from) Madeira
  (thuh) muh • thay • ruh

  (do) Porto   Port
  (thoo) paur • too

  espumante   sparkling
  ee • spoo • muhnt

  seco/doce   dry/sweet
  seh • koo/dau • seh

  tinto/branco/rosé   red/white/blush
  teen • too/bruhn • koo/raw • zeh [rosé]

  verde   dry white wine
  vehrd

Brazilian wines are produced in the southern part of the country, which turns out some good reds and whites. Labels to look for include **Almadén** and **Forestier**.

Excellent red and white aperitif and dessert wines come from the island of Madeira; **Sercial** is the driest, and **Verdelho** (medium-dry) can be drunk as an aperitif; **Boal** (or **Bual**) is smoky and less sweet than the rich dark-amber **Malvásia** (or Malsey), which is best served as a dessert wine at room temperature.

Port, famous fortified wine from the upper Douro valley, east of Oporto, is classified by vintage and blend. The vintage ports, only made in exceptional years, are harvested and left to ferment for at least two years before being bottled, and then stored for ten to twenty years. The blended ports are kept in barrels for a minimum of five years. There are two types: the younger ruby variety (**tinto aloirado**) is full-colored and full-bodied, while the tawny (**aloirado**) is less sweet, amber-colored and delicate.

Vinho verde, green wine, produced in northwest Portugal, is made from unripened grapes. It is faintly sparkling and acidic in taste, with a low alcohol content.

ON THE MENU

o abacate	avocado
oo uh • buh • <u>kaht</u>	
o abacaxi	pineapple
oo uh • buh • <u>kah</u> • shee	
a abóbora	pumpkin
uh uh • <u>baw</u> • boo • ruh	
o açafrão	saffron
oo uh • suh • <u>frohm</u>	
o acarajé	fried beans
oo uh • kuh • ruh • <u>zseh</u>	
o açúcar	sugar
oo uh • <u>soo</u> • kuhr	
o agrião	watercress
oo uh • gree • <u>ohm</u>	
a água	water
uh <u>ah</u> • gwuh	
a água de coco	coconut juice
uh <u>ah</u> • gwuh deh <u>kau</u> • koo	
a água mineral	mineral water
uh <u>ah</u> • gwuh mee • neh • <u>ral</u>	
o aipo	celery
oo ah • <u>ee</u> • poo	
a alcachofra	artichoke
uh ahl • kuh • <u>shau</u> • fruh	
as alcaparras	capers
uhz ahl • kuh • <u>pah</u> • rruhz	
o alecrim	rosemary
oo uh • leh • <u>kreeng</u>	
a aletria	sweet noodle
uh uhl • eh • <u>tree</u> • uh	pudding
a alface	lettuce
uh ahl • <u>fah</u> • seh	

à Algarvia   almond layer cake
ah uhl • guhr • vee • uh

a alheira   sausage
uh ah • lyay • ruh

o alho   garlic
oo ah • lyoo

o alho porro   leek
oo ah • lyoo pau • rroo

o almoço   lunch
oo ahl • mau • soo

as almôndegas   fishballs or
uhz ahl • mawn • deh • guhz   meatballs

o alperce   apricot
oo uhl • pehr • seh

as amêijoas   baby clams
uhz uh • may • zsoo • uhz

as ameixas   plums
uhz uh • may • shuhz

as ameixas secas   prunes
uhz uh • may • shuhz seh • kuhz

a amêndoa   almond
uh uh • mehn • doo • uh

o amendoim   peanut
oo uh • mehn • doo • eeng

a amora   blackberry
uh uh • maw • ruh

o ananás   pineapple
oo uh • nuh • nahz

a anchova   anchovy
uh uhn • shau • vuh

o aperitivo   aperitif
oo uh • pehr • uh • tee • voo

o arenque   herring
oo uh • rehn • keh

arroz
o uh • _rrauz_

rice

arroz doce
o uh • _rrauz dau_ • seh

rice pudding

assado
o uh • _sah_ • thoo

roast

atum
o uh • _toong_

tuna

aveia
h uh • _vay_ • uh

oats

avelã
h uh • veh • _luh_

hazelnut

as aves
hz _ahv_ • ehz

poultry

azeda
h uh • _zeh_ • duh

sorrel

azedo
h • _zeh_ • thoo

sour

azeite
o uh • _zay_ • teh

oil

az azeitonas
hz uh • zay • _tau_ • nuhz

olive

bacalhau
o buh • kuh • _lyahoo_

cod

bacalhau à brás
o buh • kuh • _lyahoo_
uh brahz

cod with
scrambled eggs,
onions and
shoestring potatoes

bacalhau à Conde de Guarda
o buh • kuh • _lyahoo_ uh
con • deh deh Goo • ahr • dah
Goo • ahr • dah

salt cod
creamed with
mashed potatoes

o bacalhau à Gomes de Sá
oo buh • kuh • lyahoo uh
goh • mez deh Saw

traditional cod casserole with thinly sliced potatoes, onions, garnished with hard-boiled eggs and black olives

o bacalhau dourada
oo buh • kuh • lyahoo
dou • rah • dah

cod dish served with scrambled eggs, onions and julienne potatoes

a banana
uh buh • nuh • nuh

banana

a batata
uh buh • tah • tuh

potato

a batata doce
uh buh • tah • tuh dau • seh

sweet potato

as batatas fritas
uhz buh • tah • tuhz free • tuhz

fries [chips]

o batido
oo buh • tee • thoo

milk shake

a baunilha
uh bahoo • nee • lyuh

vanilla

a bebida
uh beh • bee • thuh

drink

o berbigão
oo behr • bee • gohm

type of cockle

a beringela
uh behr • eeng • zseh • luh

eggplant [aubergine]

o besugo
oo beh • soo • goo

bream(fish)

a beterraba
uh beh • teh • rrah • buh

beet [beetroot]

o bife
oo beef

steak

o bife acebolado
oo beef uh • seh • boo • lah • thoo

steak with onions

a bola de Berlim
uh bau • luh deh behr • leeng

doughnut

a bolacha
uh boo • lah • shuh

cookie [biscuit]

a bolacha de água e sal
uh boo • lah • shuh deh ah • gwuh ee sahl

cracker

o bolinhos de bacalhau
*oo bau • leen • hos deh
buh • kuh • lyahoo*

cod fish balls

o bolo
oo bau • loo

pastry

o borrego
oo boo • rreh • goo

lamb

as broas castelares
*uhz brau • uhz
kuhz • tuh • lay • rehz*

sweet-potato cookies

as broas de mel
uh broas • uhz deh mehl

corn flour and honey
cookies

os brócolos
ooz braw • koo • looz

broccoli

o cabrito
oo kuh • bree • too

kid (goat)

a caça
uh kah • suh

game

o cacau
oo kuh • kahoo

cocoa

o cachorro quente
oo kuh • shau • roo kehnt

hot dog

o café
oo kuh • feh

coffee

o caju
oo kah • zsoo

cashew nut

a caldeirada *uh kahl • day • rah • duh*	fish stew
o caldo *oo kahl • doo*	consommé
o caldo de cana *oo kahl • doo deh kuh • nuh*	sugar-cane juice
o caldo verde *oo kahl • doo vehrd*	potato and kale soup
os camarões *ooz kuh • muh • roings*	shrimp
o canapé *oo kuh • nuh • peh*	small open sandwich
a canela *uh kuh • neh • luh*	cinnamon
a canja *uh keng • juh*	chicken soup with rice
o capão *oo cuh • pohm*	capon
o caracol *oo kuh • ruh • kawl*	snail; spiral bun with currants
o caranguejo *oo kuh • ruhn • gay • zsoo*	crab
o carapau *oo kuh • ruh • pahoo*	mackerel

o caril
oo kuh • reel

curry powder

a carne de porco
uh kahr • neh deh paur • koo

pork

a carne de sol
uh kahr • neh deh sawl

sun-dried meat, jerky

a carne de vaca
uh kahr • neh deh vah • kuh

beef

a carne picada
uh kahr • neh pee • kah • thuh

minced meat

o carneiro
oo kuhrr • nay • roo

mutton

as carnes
uhz kahr • nehz

meat

as carnes frias
uhz kahr • nehz free • uhz

[charcuterie] cold
cuts

caseiro
oo kuh • zay • roo

homemade

a castanha
uh kuhz • tuh • nyuh

chestnut

a castanha de caju
*uh kuhz • tuh • nyuh
deh kah • zsoo*

cashew nut

a (água de) Castelo
*uh (ah • gwuh deh)
kuh • steh • loo*

carbonated mineral
water

a cavala
uh kuh • vuh • luh

mackerel

a cebola
uh seh • bau • luh

onion

a cenoura
uh seh • nau • ruh

carrot

a cereja
uh seh • ray • zsuh

cherry

o chá *oo shah*	tea
o chá com leite *oo shah kaum layt*	tea with milk
o chá com limão *oo shah kaumlee • mohm*	tea with lemon
o chá de limão *oo shah deh lee • mohm*	tea made from lemon peel infusion
o chá maté *oo shah muh • teh*	tea infused with maté-tree leaf
o cherne *oo shehr • neh*	black grouper
a chicória *uh shee • kaw • ree • uh*	chicory
o chispe *oo sheez • peh*	pig's foot [trotter]
o chocolate quente *oo shoo • koo • laht kehnt*	hot chocolate
os chocos *ooz shau • kooz*	cuttlefish
o chouriço *oo shaw • ree • soo*	smoked pork sausage
o churrasco *oo shoo • rahz • koo*	charcoal-grilled meat
as cocadas *uhz caw • cah • duhz*	coconut macaroons
o coco *oo kau • koo*	coconut
a codorna *uh koo • dawrr • nuh*	quail
a codorniz *uh koo • dawrr • neez*	quail
o coelho *oo koo • eh • lyoo*	rabbit

o coentro
oo koo • ehn • troo
coriander

o cogumelo
oo koo • goo • meh • loo
button mushroom

o colorau
oo koo • loo • rahoo
paprika

os cominhos
ooz koo • mee • nyooz
cumin

a compota
uh koom • paw • tuh
compote, stewed fruit

os condimentos
ooz kaum • dee • mehn • tooz
seasonings

o congro
oo kaum • groo
conger eel

o conhaque
oo kaw • nyahk
cognac

a conta
uh kaum • tuh
bill

o copo
oo kaw • poo
glass

o coração
oo koo • ruh • sohm
heart

o cordeiro
oo koor • day • roo
lamb

a corvina
uh kawr • vee • nuh
croaker (fish)

a costeleta
uh koo • stuh • leh • tuh
cutlet

a couve
uh kaw • veh
cabbage

a couve Portuguesa
uh kaw • veh poor • too • geh • zuh
kale

a couve roxa
uh kaw • veh rau • shuh
red cabbage

a couve-de-bruxelas
uh kaw • veh de broo • sheh • luhz
brussels sprouts

a couve-flor
uh kaw • veh flaur
cauliflower

a coxinha de galinha
uh kaw • shee • nyuh deh guh • lee • nyuh
pastry filled with chicken

os cravinhos
ooz kruh • vee • nyooz
cloves

o creme
oo krehm
cream

o creme de abacate
oo krehmdeh uh • buh • kaht
avocado with lime juice and sugar

o creme leite
oo krehm layt
custard

o crepe
oo krehp
pancake

a criação
uh kree • uh • sohm
poultry

cru
kroo
raw

os crustáceos
ooz kroo • stah • see • ooz
shellfish

o damasco
oo duh • mahs • koo
apricot

a dendê
uh dehn • deh
palmoil

o doce de abóbora
oo thaus deh uh • baw • boo • ruh
pumpkin dessert

o doce de fruta
oo thaus deh froo • tuh
jam

o doce de laranja
oo thaus de luh • ruhn • zsuh
marmalade

o doce de ovos e amêndoa
oo thaus deh aw • vooz ee
uh • mehn • doo • uh
marzipan

o eiró *oo ay • raw*	eel
a empadinha *uh eem • puh • thee • nyuh*	filled pastry
o empadão de batata *oo eem • puh • dohm deh buh • tah • tuh*	shepherd's pie
a enguia *uh eng • gee • uh*	eel
o ensopado de cabrito *oo eng • soo • pah • thoo deh keh • bree • too*	kid stew
a entrada *uh ehn • trah • thuh*	appetizer [starter]
o entrecosto *oo ehn • treh • kaus • too*	sparerib
a erva-doce *uh ehr • vuh thaus*	aniseed
as ervilhas *uhz eer • vee • lyuhz*	peas
escalfado *ee • skahl • fah • thoo*	poached
o espadarte *oo ee • spah • dahr • teh*	swordfish
os espargos *ooz ees • pahr • gooz*	asparagus
o esparguete *oo ee • sparh • geht*	spaghetti
os espinafres *ooz ee • spee • nah • frehz*	spinach
estufado *ee • stoo • fah • thoo*	braised
o esturjão *oo ee • stoor • zsohm*	sturgeon
o faisão *oo feye • zohm*	pheasant

a farinha
uh fuh • ree • nyuh

flour

a farofa
uh fuh • rau • fuh

cassava flour

as favas
uhz fah • vuhz

broad beans

o feijão
oo fay • zsohm

bean

o feijão branco
oo fay • zsohm bruhn • koo

navy bean

o feijão catarino
oo fay • zsohm kuh • tuh • ree • noo

pink bean

o feijão encarnado
oo fay • zsohm eng • kuhrr • nah • thoo

red bean

o feijão frade
oo fay • zsohm frahd

black-eyed bean

o feijão guisado
oo fay • zsohm gee • sah • thoo

beans with bacon in tomato sauce

o feijão preto
oo fay • zsohm preh • too

black bean

o feijão tropeiro
oo fay • zsohm trau • pay • roo

black beans fried with jerky (Braz.)

o feijão verde
oo fay • zsohm vehrd

green beans

o fiambre
oo fee • uhm • breh

boiled ham

o fígado
oo fee • guh • doo

liver

o figo
oo fee • goo

fig

o filete
oo fee • leht

fillet of fish

o folhado
oo foo • lyah • thoo

sweet puff-pastry

as filhós
uhz fee • lyawz

fritters

a framboesa
uh fruhm • boo • eh • zuh

raspberry

o frango
oo fruhn • goo

chicken

o frango assado
oo fruhn • goo uh • sah • thoo

roast chicken

a fritada de peixe
uh free • tah • duh deh paysh

deep-fried fish

a fruta
uh froo • tuh

fruit

a fruta do conde
uh froo • tuh thoo kaum • deh

custard apple

a fruta em calda
uh froo • tuh eng kahl • duh

fruit in syrup

os frutos do mar
ooz froo • tuhz thoo mahr

seafood

a fubá
uh foo • bah

corn flour (Braz.)

a galantina
uh guh • luhn • tee • nuh

pressed meat in gelatin

o galão
oo guh • lohm

weak milky coffee

a galinha
uh guh • lee • nyuh

stewing chicken

a galinhola
uh guh • lee • nyaw • luh

woodcock

as gambas
uhz guhm • buhz

shrimp [king prawns]

o ganso
oo guhn • soo

goose

a garoupa
uh guh • rauoo • puh

large grouper (fish)

a garrafa
uh guh • <u>rrah</u> • fuh
bottle

a gasosa
uh guh • <u>zaw</u> • zuh
lemonade

o gaspacho
oo guhz • <u>pah</u> • shoo
chilled soup

o gelado
oo zseh • <u>lah</u> • thoo
ice cream

a gelatina
uh zseh • luh • <u>tee</u> • nuh
jelly

o gelo
oo <u>zseh</u> • loo
ice

o gengibre
oo zsehn • <u>zsee</u> • breh
ginger

os grelos
ooz <u>greh</u> • looz
turnip sprouts

a groselha
uh groo • <u>zeh</u> • lyuh
red currant

o guisado
oo gee • <u>zah</u> • thoo
stew

a hortaliça
uh awr • tuh • <u>lee</u> • suh
fresh vegetables

a hortelã
uh awr • teh • <u>luh</u>
mint

o inhame
oo ee • <u>nuhm</u>
yam

oo iogurte
oo yaw • <u>goort</u>
yogurt

a isca de peixe
uh <u>ees</u> • kuh deh <u>paysh</u>
fried small fish (Braz.)

as iscas
uhz <u>ees</u> • kuhz
sliced liver

a jabuticaba
uh juh • boo • tee • <u>cah</u> • buh
type of cherry (Braz.)

a jardineira
uh zsuhr • dee • nay • ruh

mixed vegetables

o javali
oo zsuh • vah • li

wild boar

o kibe
oo keeb

meat and bulgur croquette (Braz.)

o kiwi
oo kee • vee

kiwi

a lagosta
uh lah • gau • stuh

lobster

o lagostim
oo luh • gau • steeng

crayfish

lagostim do-rio
luh • gau • steeng doo ree • oo

fresh-water crayfish

a lampreia
uh luhm • pray • uh

lamprey

a laranja
uh luh • ruhn • zsuh

orange

a laranjada
uh luh • ruhn • zsah • thuh

orange soda

o lavagante
oo luh • vu • guhnt

lobster

a lebre
uh leh • breh

hare

os legumes
ooz leh • goomz

vegetables

o leite
oo layt

milk

o leite de coco
oo layt deh kau • koo

coconut milk

o leitão
oo lay • tohm

suckling pig

as lentilhas
uhz lehn • tee • lyuhz

lentils

a lima
uh <u>lee</u> • muh
lime

o limão
oo lee • <u>mohm</u>
lemon

o limão verde
oo lee • <u>mohm</u> vehrd
lime (Braz.)

a língua
uh <u>leen</u> • gwuh
tongue

o linguado
oo leen • <u>gwah</u> • doo
sole

a linguiça
uh leen • <u>gwee</u> • suh
thin sausage

o lombo
oo <u>laum</u> • boo
loin

o louro
oo <u>lau</u> • roo
bay leaf

a lula
uh <u>loo</u> • luh
squid

a maçã
uh muh • <u>suh</u>
apple

o maçapão
oo muh • suh • <u>pohm</u>
marzipan

o macarrão
oo muh • kuh • <u>rrohm</u>
macaroni

maduro
muh • <u>thoo</u> • roo
ripe

a maionese
uh meye • aw • <u>nehz</u>
mayonnaise

a malagueta
uh muh • luh • <u>geh</u> • tuh
hot pepper

o mamão
oo muh • <u>mohm</u>
papaya

a manga
uh <u>muhn</u> • guh
mango

o manjericão
oo muhn • zsehr • ee • kohm
basil

a manteiga
uh muhn • tay • guh
butter

o maracujá
oo muh • ruh • koo • zsah
passion fruit

os mariscos
ooz muh • rees • kooz
seafood

a marmelada
uh muhr • meh • lah • duh
thick quince paste

a massa
uh mah • suh
pasta; dough; pastry

o massapão
oo muh • suh • pohm
marzipan

os massapães
ooz muh • suh • pengz
almond macaroons

o mate
oo maht
tea with maté leaf

o medalhão
oo meh • deh • lyohm
tenderloin steak

o medronho
oo meh • drau • nyoo
arbutus berry (small strawberry-like fruit)

o mel
oo mehl
honey

a melancia
uh muh • luhn • see • uh
watermelon

o melão
oo meh • lohm
melon

o melão com presunto
oo meh • lohm kaumpreh • zoon • too
melon with ham

o mero
oo meh • roo
red grouper (fish)

a mexerica
uh meh • sheh • ree • kuh
tangerine

os mexilhões
ooz meh • shee • lyoings

mussels

as migas de bacalhau
uhz mee • guhz deh buh • kuh • lyahoo

dried cod soup

o milho
oo mee • lyoo

sweet corn

os miolos
ooz mee • aw • looz

brains

o misto quente
oo mee • stoo kehnt

ham-and-cheese toasted sandwich

o morango
oo moo • ruhn • goo

strawberry

a morcela
uh moor • seh • luh

blood sausage [black pudding]

a mortadela
uh moor • tuh • deh • luh

mortadella

a mostarda
uh moo • stahr • duh

mustard

a mousse de chocolate
uh moo • seh deh shoo • koo • laht

chocolate pudding

a mousse de maracujá
uh moo • seh deh muh • ruh • koo • zsah

passion fruit mousse

as nabiças
uhz nuh • bee • suhz

turnip greens

os nabos
ooz nah • booz

turnips

a nata
uh nah • tuh

fresh cream

a nata batida
uh nah • tuh buh • tee • duh

whipped cream

(ao) natural
(ahoo) nuh • too • rahl

plain

as nêsperas
uhz neh • speh • ruhz

loquat (fruit)

no forno *noo <u>faurr</u> • noo*	baked
a noz *uh nawz*	nut
a noz moscada *uh nawz moo • <u>skah</u> • thuh*	nutmeg
o óleo *oo <u>aw</u> • lee • oo*	oil
o óleo de amendoim *oo <u>aw</u> • lee • oo deh uh • mehn • doo • <u>eeng</u>*	peanut oil
a omelete *uh aw • meh • <u>leht</u>*	omelet
o orégão *oo aw • reh • <u>gohm</u>*	oregano
o osso *oo <u>au</u> • soo*	bone
a ostra *uh <u>aw</u> • struh*	oyster
o ovo *oo <u>aw</u> • voo*	egg
os ovos cozidos *ooz <u>aw</u> • vooz koo • <u>zee</u> • thooz*	boiled eggs
os ovos escalfados *ooz <u>aw</u> • vooz ees • kahl • <u>fah</u> • thooz*	poached eggs
os ovos estrelados *ooz <u>aw</u> • vooz ees • truh • <u>lah</u> • dooz*	fried eggs
os ovos mexidos *ooz <u>aw</u> • vooz meh • <u>shee</u> • dooz*	scrambled eggs
os ovos quentes *ooz <u>aw</u> • vooz kehntz*	soft-boiled eggs
panado *puh • <u>nah</u> • thoo*	breaded

a panqueca
uh puhn • keh • kuh
pancake

o pão (escuro/integral)
oo pohm
(ees • koo • roo/een • teh • grahl)
bread (brown/whole wheat)

o pão de centeio
oo pohmdeh sehn • tay • oo
rye bread

o pão-de-ló
oo pohm • deh • law
coffee cake

o pãozinho
oo pohm • zee • nyoo
bread roll

o pargo
oo pahr • goo
bream(fish)

as passas (de uva)
uhz pah • suhz (deh oo • vuh)
raisin

passado
puh • sah • thoo
cooked (meat, etc.)

o pastel
oo puhs • tehl
small pie

pastéis de Bélem
oo puhs • tehl
small custard tartlets, famous in Lisbon

o pato
oo pah • too
duck

o peito de galinha
oo pay • too deh guh • lee • nyuh
chicken breast

o peixe
oo paysh
fish

o peixe-agulha
oo paysh • uh • goo • lya
garfish

o peixe-espada
oo paysh ees • pah • duh
swordfish

o pepino
oo peh • pee • noo
cucumber

o **pepino de conserva**
oo peh • _pee_ • noo deh kaum • _sehr_ • vuh — pickle [gherkin]

a **pêra**
uh _peh_ • ruh — pear

a **perca**
uh _pehr_ • kuh — perch

a **perdiz**
uh pehr • _deez_ — partridge

a **perna de galinha**
uh _pehrr_ • nuh deh guh • _lee_ • nyuh — chicken leg

o **pernil**
oo perr • _neel_ — ham

o **pêro**
oo _peh_ • rau — variety of apple

o **peru**
oo peh • _roo_ — turkey

os **pés de porco**
ooz pehz deh _paur_ • koo — pig's feet [trotters]

a **pescada**
uh pehz • _kah_ • thuh — whiting

o **pêssego**
oo _peh_ • suh • goo — peach

os **petiscos**
ooz peh • _tees_ • kooz — appetizers [starters]

a **pevide**
uh peh • _veed_ — salted pumpkin seed

os **pickles**
ooz _pee_ • kehlz — pickled vegetables

a **pimenta**
uh pee • _mehn_ • tuh — pepper

os **pimentos assados**
ooz pee • _mehn_ • tooz uh • _sah_ • dooz — roasted peppers

o **pinhão**
oo pee • _nyohm_ — nut

a pinhoada
uh pee • nyoo • ah • duh

pine nut brittle

o pipis
oo pee • peez

spicy giblet stew

o piri-piri
oo pee • ree pee • ree

seasoning of hot chili
pepper and olive oil

o polvo
oo paul • voo

octopus

o pombo
oo paum • boo

pigeon

o porco
oo paur • koo

pork

a posta
uh paws • tuh

slice of fish or meat

o presunto
oo preh • zoon • too

cured ham

o presunto cru
oo preh • zoon • too kroo

dried ham

o pudim flan
oo poo • deeng fluhn

caramel custard

o puré de batatas
oo poo • reh deh buh • tah • tuhz

mashed potatoes

a queijada
uh kay • zsah • duh

small cottage-
cheese tart

o queijinho do céu
oo kay • zsee • nyoo doo sehoo

marzipan balls rolled
in sugar

o queijo
oo kay • zsoo

cheese

o quiabo
oo kee • ah • boo

okra

a rabanada
uh ruh • buh • nah • duh

French toast

o rabanete
oo ruh • buh • neht

radish

a raia
uh <u>reye</u> • uh

skate (fish)

a rainha-cláudia
uh ray • <u>ee</u> • nyuh <u>klaw</u> • dee • uh

greengage plum

recheado
eh • shee • <u>ah</u> • thoo

stuffed

o recheio
oo re • <u>shay</u> • oo

stuffing

o refogado
oo reh • foo • <u>gah</u> • thoo

onions fried in olive oil

o refresco
oo reh • <u>frehs</u> • koo

soft drink

o repolho
oo rreh • <u>pau</u> • lyoo

cabbage

o rim
oo rreeng

kidney

o robalo
oo <u>rraw</u> • buh • loo

sea bass

o rodízio
oo rroo • <u>dee</u> • zee • oo

selection of chargrilled meats (Braz.)

a romã
uh rrau • <u>muh</u>

pomegranate

a rosca
uh rraus • kuh
ring-shaped white bread

o rosmaninho
oo rrooz • muh • neeng • nyoo
rosemary

o ruivo
oo rroo • ee • voo
red gurnard (fish)

o sal
oo sahl
salt

a salada
uh suh • lah • duh
salad

a salada de alface/escarola
uh suh • lah • duh deh ahl • fah • seh/ees • kuh • raw • luh
green salad

a salada de agrião
uh suh • lah • duh deh uh • gree • ohm
watercress salad

a salada mista
uh suh • lah • duh mees • tuh
tomato and lettuce salad

salgado
sahl • gah • thoo
salted

o salmão (fumado)
oo suh • mohm (foo • mah • thoo)
(smoked) salmon

o salmonete
oo sahl • moo • neht
red mullet

a salsa
uh sahl • suh
parsley

a salsicha
uh sahl • see • shuh
sausage

salteado
sahl • tee • ah • thoo
sautéed

a salva
uh sahl • vuh
sage

as sandes
uhz suhndz
sandwich

a sanduíche _uh suhn • doo • eesh_	sandwich
a santola _uh suhn • taw • luh_	spider-crab
o sarapatel _oo suh • ruh • puh • tehl_	pork or mutton stew
a sarda _uh sahr • thuh_	mackerel
as sardinhas _uhz suhr • dee • nyuhz_	sardines
o sável _oo sah • vehl_	shad (herring-like fish)
seco _seh • koo_	dry
a sêmola _uh seh • moo • luh_	semolina
o sericá alentejano _oo seh • ree • kah_ _uh • lehn • teh • zsuh • noo_	cinnamon soufflé
a sidra _uh see • druh_	cider
as sobremesas _uhz sau • breh • meh • zuhz_	dessert
a solha _uh sau • lyuh_	plaice (fish)
o sonho _oo sau • nyoo_	type of doughnut
a sopa _uh sau • puh_	soup
o sumo _oo soo • moo_	fruit juice
o suspiro _oo soo • spee • roo_	meringue
a taínha _uh tah • ee • nyuh_	gray mullet (fish)

a tâmara
uh tuh • muh • ruh

date

a tangerina
uh tuhn • zsuh • ree • nuh

tangerine

a tarte de amêndoa
uh tahrt de uh • mehn • doo • uh

almond tart

o tempero
oo tehm • peh • roo

seasoning

tenro
tehn • rroo

tender

o tomate
oo too • maht

tomato

o tomilho
oo too • mee • lyoo

thyme

a toranja
uh tau • ruhn • zsuh

grapefruit

as torradas
uhz too • rrah • duhz

toast

o torrão de ovos
oo too • rrohm deh aw • vooz

marzipan candy

a tosta
uh taw • stuh

toasted sandwich

o toucinho
oo tau • see • nyoo

bacon

o tremoço
oo treh • maw • soo

salted lupin bean

a trufa
uh troo • fuh

truffle

a truta
uh troo • tuh

trout

o tutano
oo too • tuh • noo

marrow

as uvas
uhz oo • vuhz

grapes

as vagens
uhz vah • gehnz   green beans

variado
vuh • ree • ah • thoo   assorted

o veado
oo vee • ah • thoo   venison

os vegetais variados
ooz veh • zseh • teyez   mixed vegetables
vuh • ree • ah • thooz

a vieira
uh vee • ay • ruh   scallop

o vinagre
oo vee • nah • greh   vinegar

a vitela
uh vee • tehl • uh   veal

PEOPLE

| GOING OUT | 230 |
| ROMANCE | 234 |

GOING OUT

NEED TO KNOW

What is there to do in the evenings?	**O que há para se fazer à noite?** *oo keh ah puh • ruh seh fuh • zehr ah noyt*
Do you have a program of events?	**Tem um programa dos espectáculos?** *teng oong proo • gruh • muh dooz ee • spehk • tah • koo • looz*
What's playing at the movies [cinema] tonight?	**O que há no cinema hoje à noite?** *oo kee ah noo see • neh • muh auzseh ah noyt*
Where's...?	**Onde é...?** *aund eh...*
the downtown area	**o centro** *oo sehn • troo*
the bar	**o bar** *oo bar*
the dance club	**a discoteca** *uh deez • koo • teh • kuh*
Is there a cover charge?	**É preciso pagar entrada?** *eh preh • see • zoo puh • gahr ehn • trah • duh*

ENTERTAINMENT

Can you recommend...?	**Pode recomendar-me...?** *pawd reh • koo • mehn • dahr • meh...*
a concert	**um concerto** *oong kaun • sehr • too*

a movie	**um filme**
	oong <u>feel</u> • meh
an opera	**uma ópera**
	oo • muh <u>aw</u> • peh • ruh
a play	**um teatro**
	oong tee • <u>ah</u> • troo
When does it start/ end?	**A que horas começa/acaba?**
	uh kee <u>aw</u> • ruhz koo • <u>meh</u> • suh/ uh • <u>kah</u> • buh
What's the dress code?	**O que é o código de vestido?**
	oo kee eh oo <u>kaw</u> • dee • goo deh vehs • <u>tee</u> • thoo
I like…	**Gosto de…**
	<u>gaws</u> • too deh…
classical music	**música clássica**
	<u>moo</u> • zee • kuh <u>klah</u> • see • kuh
folk music	**música popular**
	<u>moo</u> • zee • kuh poo • poo • <u>lahr</u>

Carnaval is widely celebrated both in Portugal and Brazil. A time of lavish celebration before Lent, **Carnaval** begins four days before Ash Wednesday, and ends with the famous 'Fat Tuesday' celebration. Look for parades on the streets and carnival balls (**bailes carnavalescos**). The famed **Carnaval do Rio** sees the spectacularly colorful competition between the various samba schools in a parade through the streets of Rio de Janeiro.

Samba and bossa nova are the dance styles best known abroad, but regional rhythms like **pagode**, **lambada**, **frevo**, **forró**, **maracatu**, **baião**, **carimbó** and **bumba-meu boi**, with their mixture of African, Indian, and European influences, are also very popular with both locals and tourists.

jazz	**jazz**
	zsahz
pop music	**pop**
	pawp
rap	**rap**
	rahp

For Tickets, see page 46.

A popular evening activity in Portugal is a visit to a
casa de fados (house of blues), an intimate, late-night
restaurant where your meal is accompanied by the melodies
of the **fado**, the national folk song.
Local papers and weekly entertainment guides—such as
Sete will tell you what is going on.

YOU MAY HEAR...

Desligue os seus telefones móveis, **por favor.** *dehz • lee • geh* *oohz sehooz tehl • fawnz maw • vayz poor fuh • vaur*	Turn off your cell [mobile] phones, please.

NIGHTLIFE

What is there to do in the evenings?	**O que há para se fazer à noite?** *oo keh ah puh • ruh seh fuh • zehr ah noyt*
Can you recommend...?	**Pode recomendar-me...?** *pawd reh • koo • mehn • dahr • meh...*
a bar	**um bar** *oong bar*

a casino	**um casino**
	oong kuh • <u>see</u> • noo
a dance club	**uma discoteca**
	oo • muh dee • skoo • <u>teh</u> • kuh
a gay club	**um clube gay**
	oong kloob gay
a jazz club	**um clube de jazz**
	oong kloob deh zsahz
a club with Portuguese music?	**uma discoteca com música Portuguesa?**
	oo • muh dee • skoo • <u>teh</u> • kuh kaum moo • zee • kuh poor • too • gehza
Is there live music?	**Há música ao vivo?**
	ah <u>moo</u> • zee • kuh ahoo <u>vee</u> • voo
How do I get there?	**Como é que vou até lá?**
	<u>kau</u> • moo eh keh vauoo uh • <u>teh</u> lah
Is there a cover charge?	**É preciso pagar entrada?**
	eh preh • <u>see</u> • zoo puh • <u>gahr</u> ehn • <u>trah</u> • duh
Let's go dancing.	**Vamos dançar.**
	<u>vuh</u> • mooz duhn • <u>sahr</u>
Is this area safe at night?	**Esta zona é segura à noite?**
	eh • stuh zau • nuh eh seh • goo • ruh ah noyt?

i

Portugal offers the usual range of nightclubs along the coast; most don't begin to get lively until around midnight.

ROMANCE

NEED TO KNOW

Would you like to go out for a drink/dinner?	**Queres ir tomar uma bebida/comer fóra?**
	keh • rehz eer too • _mahr_ oo • muh beh • _bee_ • thuh/koo • mehr _faw_ • ruh
What are your plans for tonight/tomorrow?	**Quais são os seus planos para hoje à noite/amanhã?**
	kweyez sohm ooz sehooz _pluh_ • nooz puh • ruh auzseh ah noyt/uh • muh • _nyuh_
Can I have your number?	**Podes dar-me o teu número de telefone?**
	pawd • ehz _dahr_ • meh oo tehoo _noo_ • meh • roo deh tehl • _fawn_
Can I join you?	**Posso acompanhar-te?**
	paw • soo uh • kaum • puh • _nyahr_ • teh
Can I buy you a drink?	**O que quer beber?**
	oo keh kehr beh • _behr_
I like you.	**Gosto de ti**
	gawzh • too deh tee
I love you.	**Amo-te.**
	_uh_ • moo teh

THE DATING GAME

Would you like to go out for...?	**Queres ir sair para...?**
	kehrz eer seh • eer _puh_ • ruh...
coffee	**um café**
	oong kuh • _feh_
a drink	**uma bebida**
	_oo_ • muh beh • _bee_ • thuh

dinner	**jantar**
	zsuhn • <u>tahr</u>
What are your plans for…?	**Quais são os seus planos para…?**
	kweyez sohm ooz sehooz <u>pluh</u> • nooz <u>puh</u> • ruh…
tonight	**hoje à noite**
	auzseh ah noyt
tomorrow	**amanhã**
	uh • muh • <u>nyuh</u>
this weekend	**este fim de semana**
	ehst feeng deh seh • <u>muh</u> • nuh
Where would you like to go?	**Onde queres ir?**
	aund kehrz eer
I'd like to go to…	**Quero ir à…**
	<u>keh</u> • roo eer ah…
Do you like…?	**Gosta de…?**
	<u>gaw</u> • stuh deh…
Can I have your number/e-mail?	**Podes dar-me o teu número de telefone/e-mail?**
	<u>pawd</u> • ehz <u>dahr</u> • meh oo tehoo <u>noo</u> • meh • roo deh tehl • <u>fawn</u>/ee • <u>mehl</u>
Are you on Facebook/Twitter?	**Está no Facebook/Twitter?**
	ee • stah noo Facebook/Twitter

Can I join you?	**Posso acompanhar-te?**
	paw • soo uh • kaum • puh • _nyahr_ • teh
You look great!	**Está linda!**
	ee • _stah_ _leen_ • duh
Let's go somewhere quieter.	**Vamos para um sítio mais sossegado.**
	vuh • mooz _puh_ • ruh oong _see_ • tyoo meyez soo • seh • _gah_ • thoo

For Communications, see page 87.

ACCEPTING & REJECTING

I'd love to.	**Adorava ir.**
	uh • daw • _rah_ • vuh eer
Where should we meet?	**Onde nos vamos encontrar?**
	aund nooz _vuh_ • mooz ehng • kaun • _trahr_
I'll meet you at the bar/ your hotel.	**Vou ter contigo ao bar/hotel.**
	vauoo tehr kaun • _tee_ • goo ahoo bahr/ _aw_ • tehl
I'll come by at…	**Eu passo por lá às…**
	ehoo _pah_ • soo poor lah ahz…
What's your address?	**Qual é a sua morada?**
	kwahl eh uh _soo_ • uh maw • _rah_ • duh
I'm busy.	**Mas tenho imenso que fazer.**
	muhz _teh_ • nyoo ee • _mehn_ • soo keh fuh • _zehr_
I'm not interested.	**Não estou interessado m/interessada f.**
	nohm ee • _stawoo_ een • treh • _sah_ • thoo/ een • treh • _sah_ • thuh
Leave me alone.	**Deixe-me em paz.**
	day • sheh • meh eng pahz
Stop bothering me!	**Está quieto!**
	ee • _stah_ kee • _eh_ • too

GETTING INTIMATE

Can I hug/kiss you?	**Posso dar-te um abraço/beijo?**	
	paw • soo _dahr_ • teh oong uh • _brah_ • soo/ _bay_ • zsoo	
Yes.	**Sim.**	
	seeng	
No.	**Não.**	
	nohm	
Stop!	**Pára!**	
	pah • ruh	
I love you.	**Amo-te.**	
	_uh_ • moo teh	

SEXUAL PREFERENCES

Are you gay?	**Ès homossexual?**	
	ehz aw • maw • _sehk_ • soo • ahl	
I'm...	**Sou...**	
	sauoo...	
heterosexual	**heterossexual**	
	eh • teh • raw • _sehk_ • soo • ahl	
homosexual	**homossexual**	
	aw • maw • _sehk_ • soo • ahl	
bisexual	**bissexual**	
	bee • _sehk_ • soo • ahl	
Do you like men/ women?	**Gosta de homens/mulheres?**	
	gaw • stuh deh _aw_ • mengz/moo • _lyehrz_	

DICTIONARY

ENGLISH–
PORTUGUESE   240

PORTUGUESE–
ENGLISH   265

ENGLISH–PORTUGUESE

A

abbey a abadia
able capaz
about àcerca de
above acima
abroad no estrangeiro
abscess o abcesso
accept aceitar
access o acesso
accident o acidente
accidentally sem querer
accommodation o alojamento
accompany acompanhar
accountant o contabilista
activity a actividade
across do outro lado
adaptor o adaptador
address o endereço, a morada
admission charge o preço de entrada
adult o adulto
aerobics aeróbica
after depois
afternoon tarde
aftershave a loção para depois da barba
after-sun lotion a loção para depois do sol
age a idade
ago há
agree concordar
air conditioning o ar condicionado
air mattress o colchão pneumático
air pump a máquina pneumática
airline a linha aérea
airmail a via aérea
airport o aeroporto
aisle seat o lugar na coxia
alarm clock o despertador
alcoholic drink a bebida alcoólica
all tudo
allergic alérgico
allergy a alergia
allow permitir
almost quase
alone sózinho
already já
also também
alter modificar
alternate route a rota

adj adjective	**BE** British English	**prep** preposition
adv adverb	**n** noun	**v** verb

alternada

aluminum foil o papel de alumínio

always sempre

ambassador o embaixador

ambulance a ambulância

American o americano, a americana

anesthetic a anestesia

and e

announcement anúncio

another outro, outra

answer atender

antibiotic o antibiótico

antifreeze o anticongelante

antique a antiguidade

antiseptic cream a pomada antiséptica

any algum

anyone else mais alguém

anyone alguém

anything alguma coisa

apartment o apartamento

apologize pedir desculpa

apology a desculpa

appointment o apontamento

approximately aproximadamente

archery o tiro ao arco

architect o arquitecto, a arquitecta

architecture a arquitectura

area a área

area code o indicativo

around (the corner) ao virar da esquina

arrange arranjar

arrivals (airport) as chegadas

arrive chegar

art a arte

art gallery a galeria de arte

artificial sweetener o adoçante

artist o/a artista

ashtray o cinzeiro

ask pedir

asleep adormecido, adormecida

aspirin a aspirina

at least pelo menos

athletics atletismo

attack o ataque

attendant o empregado, a empregada

attractive atraente

aunt a tia

Australia a Austrália

Australian o australiano, a australiana

authentic autêntico

authenticity autenticidade

automatic (car) o carro de mudanças automáticas

automatic teller machine (ATM) o multibanco

avalanche a avalanche

away longe

awful horrível

B

baby o bebé; ~sitter baby-sitter; ~wipes os toalhetes de limpeza para o bebé
baby bottle o biberom
back as costas
bachache a dor de costas
backpack a mochila
bacon toucinho
bad mau, má
bakery a padaria
balcony a varanda
ball a bola
ballet o ballet
band (musical) a banda musical
bandage a ligadura
bank o banco
bar o bar
barber o barbeiro
baseball basebol
basement a cave
basin a bacia
basket o cesto
basketball basquetebol
bath o banho
bathe tomar banho
bathroom a casa de banho
battery a pilha; ~ (car, computer) a bateria
battle site o campo de batalha
be v ser; ~ (temporary state) estar; ~ (location) ficar

beach a praia
beard a barba
beautiful bonito, bonita
because porque; ~ of por causa de
bed a cama; ~ and breakfast quarto e pequeno-almoço
bedding a roupa de cama
bedroom o quarto (de dormir)
bee a abelha
beer a cerveja
before antes de
begin v começar
beginner o/a principiante
beginning o começo
beige beige
belong pertencer
belt o cinto
best melhor
better melhor
between entre
bib a babete
bicycle a bicicleta
big grande
bigger o/a maior
bikini o bikini
binoculars os binóculos
bird o pássaro
bishop o bispo
bite (insect) a picada (de insecto)
bitter azedo
bizarre estranho
black preto

blanket o cobertor
bleach a lixívia
blouse a blusa
blow-dry o secador
blue azul
blueberry o mirtilo
board embarcar
boarding (plane) embarque
boarding pass cartão de embarque
boat o barco
boiled cozido
book n o livro
book v reservar
book of tickets a caderneta de bilhetes
bookstore a livraria
boots as botas
border a fronteira
boring aborrecido
botanical garden o jardim botânico
bottle a garrafa; ~ **opener** o abre-garrafas
bowl a malga
box office a bilheteira
boxing o boxe
boy o rapaz
boyfriend o namorado
bra o sutiã
bracelet a pulseira
brake n o travão
brass o latão
Brazil o Brasil
Brazilian brasileiro

bread o pão
break v partir
breakdown avariar
break-in o assalto
breakfast o pequeno-almoço
breathe v respirar
bridge a ponte
briefcase a pasta
briefs as calcinhas
brilliant brilhante
bring v trazer
Britain a Grã-Bretanha
British britânico
brochure o folheto
bronze o bronze
brother o irmão
brown o castanho
brush a escova
bucket (pail) o balde
build v construir
building o edifício
built construído
burger o hambúrguer
burglary o roubo
burnt queimado
bus o autocarro; ~ **(long-distance)** a camioneta; ~ **station** a estação de autocarros; ~ **stop** a paragem de autocarro
business class (em) business; ~ **a trip** viagem de negócios
business card o cartão
busy ocupado

but mas
butcher shop o talho
butter a manteiga
button o botão
buy v comprar
bye adeus

C

cabin a cabina
cable car o funicular; o teleférico
café o café
cake o bolo
calendar o calendário
call v chamar
camcorder a câmara de vídeo
camera a máquina fotográfica; ~ **case** o estojo para a máquina; ~ **store** a loja de artigos fotográficos
camp v acampar
camping campismo; ~ **equipment** o material de campismo
campsite o parque de campismo
can n a lata; ~ **opener** o abre-latas
Canadá o Canadá
Canadian canadiano
canal o canal
cancel v cancelar
cancer (disease) o cancro
candle a vela
candy os rebuçados

canoe a canoa
canoeing fazer canoagem
canyon o desfiladeiro
car o carro; ~ **hire [BE]** aluguer de carros; ~ **park [BE]** o parque de estacionamento; ~ **rental** aluguer de carros
carafe o jarro
card o cartão; **ATM** ~ o cartão multibanco; **credit** ~ o cartão de crédito; **debit** ~ o cartão de débito; **phone** ~ o cartão de chamadas
cards as cartas
carpet o tapete
carry transportar
carry-on levar
carton o pacote
cash o dinheiro
cash v cobrar
casino o casino
castle o castelo
cat o gato
catch v (**bus**) apanhar o autocarro
cathedral a catedral
cause v causar
cave a caverna
CD o CD
CD-player o leitor de CDs
cell phone o telemóvel
celcius celsius
cemetery o cemitério
cent o cêntimo
certificate o certificado

chair a cadeira

change n (coins) trocado; ~ v (bus) mudar (de autocarro); ~ v (clothes) trocar (de roupa); ~ v (money) trocar dinheiro; ~ v (reservation) mudar a reserva

changing rooms os vestiários

channel (sea) o canal

chapel a capela

charcoal o carvão

charge a tarifa

cheap barato

cheaper mais barato

check (bill) a conta; put it on the ~ ponha na conta

check v verificar

checkbook o livro de cheques

check-in desk o balcão de registo

check out v (hotel) pagar a conta

checking account a conta corrente

checkout (supermarket) a caixa

cheers à sua saúde

cheese o queijo

chemical toilet a fossa séptica

chemist [BE] a farmácia

chickenpox a varicela

child o menino

child's seat a cadeirinha de criança; ~ (in car) a cadeira de criança

chips [BE] as batatas fritas

church a igreja

cigarette o cigarro

cigars os charutos

cinema o cinema

class a classe

clean adj limpo

clean v limpar

cleaner (person) o empregado da limpeza; ~ (product) o produto de limpeza

cliff a falésia

cling film [BE] o papel aderente

clock o relógio

close (near) perto

close v fechar

clothes a roupa; ~ dryer a máquina de secar

clothing store a loja de artigos de vestuário

cloudy nublado

clubs (golf) os tacos de golfe

coast a costa

coat o casaco

cockroach a barata

coffee o café

coin a moeda

cold frio; ~ (illness) a constipação

colleague o colega

college o colégio

color a cor

comb o pente

comedy a comédia

comforter o edredão

commission a comissão
compartment (train) o compartimento
compass o compasso
complain reclamar
complaint a reclamação
computer o computador
conditioner (hair) o amaciador para o cabelo
condom o preservativo
conductor (orchestra) o maestro
conference a conferência
confirm v confirmar
confirmation a confirmação
connect ligar
connection (flight) ligação
conscious consciente
constipation a prisão de ventre
consulate o consulado
contact v contactar
contact lens as lentes de contacto
contain v conter
contagious contagioso
contraceptive o contraceptivo
convenient conveniente
cook o cozinheiro, a cozinheira
cook v cozinhar
cool (temperature) fresco
copper o cobre
corkscrew o saca-rolhas
corn o milho
corner a esquina
correct correcto

cost o custo
cot a cama de bebé, o berço
cotton o algodão
cough n a tosse; ~ v tossir
country (nation) o país
countryside o campo
couple (pair) o par
course (meal) o prato
cousin o primo
crash n (car) o desastre
credit card o cartão de crédito; ~ **number** o número do cartão de crédito
cross v (road) atravessar
crowded com muita gente
cruise o cruzeiro
crystal o cristal
cup a chávena
cupboard o armário
currency a moeda
currency exchange (office) loja de câmbio
customs a alfândega; ~ **declaration** declaração da alfândega
cut n o corte; ~ v cortar
cycling [BE] o ciclismo

D

daily diariamente
damage avariado
damp húmido
dance n a dança; ~ v dançar; ~ **club** o clube de dansa
dangerous perigoso

dark escuro
daughter filha
dawn a madrugada
day o dia
dead morto; ~
  (battery) descarregada
deaf surdo
debit card (Port) o cartão de
  débito
deck chair a cadeira de
  encosto
declare v declarar
decline o declínio
deduct v **(money)** deduzir
deep profundo
degrees (temperature) os
  graus
delay o atraso
delete (computer) apagar
delicatessen a charcutaria
delicious delicioso
deliver v entregar
denim a ganga
dental floss o fio dental
dentist o dentista
deodorant o desodorizante
depart v **(train, bus)** partida
department store o grande
  armazém
departure (train) a partida
depend depende
deposit n o depósito
deposit v depositar
destination o destino
detergent detergente

diabetes os diabetes
diabetic o diabético
diamonds os diamantes
diaper a fralda
diarrhea a diarreia
dictionary o dicionário
diesel o gasóleo [diesel]
difficult difícil
digital digital
dining room a sala de jantar
dinner o jantar
direct adj directo
direct v indicar
direction a direcção
directory (telephone) a lista
  telefónica
dirty sujo, suja
disabled (person) o/a
  deficiente
disconnect (computer)
  desligar
discount o desconto
dish (meal) o prato
dishes a louça
dishwashing liquid o
  detergente para a louça
display case a vitrina
disposable (camera)
  máquina descartável
dive v mergulhar
divorced divorciado
doctor o médico
dog o cão
doll a boneca
dollar (U.S.) o dólar

domestic (flight) domestico
door a porta
double bed a cama de casal
double room o quarto duplo
down abaixo
downstairs em baixo
downtown o centro da cidade
dozen dúzia
dress n **(clothing)** vestido
drink n bebida
drinking water água potável
drive v conduzir
driver condutor
driver's license a carta de condução
drugstore a farmácia
drunk o bêbado
dry cleaner a lavandaria de limpeza a seco
during durante
dusty poeirento
duty (tax) dever
duty-free goods a mercadoria isenta de taxas
duty-free shopping as compras duty-free

E

ear o ouvido
ear drops gotas para os ouvidos
earlier mais cedo
early cedo
earrings os brincos

east leste
easy fácil
eat comer
economy class a classe económica
electricity a electricidade
elevator o elevador
e-mail n o email; v enviar emails
e-mail address morada de email
embassy a embaixada
emerald a esmeralda
emergency a emergência; ~ **exit** a saída de emergência
empty adj vazio
enamel (jewelry) esmalte
end v terminar
engine o motor
England a Inglaterra
English inglês
enjoy v apreciar
enough bastante
enter entrar
entertainment entretenimento
envelope o envelope
equipment (sports) o equipamento (desportivo)
erase v apagar
error o erro
escalator a escada rolante
essential essencial
e-ticket o bilhete electrónico
EU (European Union) a

UE (União Europeia)
euro o euro
Europe a Europa
except excepto
excess o excesso
exchange v trocar
exchange rate a taxa de câmbio
excursion a excursão
excuse me (apology) desculpe-me; **(to get attention)** desculpe
exhausted adj exausto
exhibition a exposição
exit a saída
expensive caro
expiration date a data de validade
extremely extremamente
eye o olho

F

face a cara
facial a limpeza de pele
family a família
famous famoso
fan (electric) a ventoinha
far longe
fare o bilhete
farm a quinta
fast depressa
faster mais rápido
fast food as refeições rápidas
fat n a gordura; adj gordo
fat-free sem gordura

father o pai
faucet a torneira
favorite o preferido, a preferida
fax n o fax
fax v enviar fax
fear o medo
feed v alimentar
female a mulher
ferry o ferry
few poucos
fever a febre
field (sports) o campo
fill out v (form) preencher
film (camera) o filme
fine (penalty) a multa
fire n o fogo
fire alarm o alarme de incêndio
fire department [brigade] os bombeiros
fire escape a saída de incêndio
fire extinguisher o extintor de incêndio
first o primeiro
first class a primeira classe
first-aid kit o estojo de primeiros socorros
fit (clothes) servir
fitting room o gabinete de provas
fix v arranjar
flag a bandeira
flash (photography) o flash
flashlight a lanterna
flat (tire) o furo
flight o vôo

floor (level) o andar
flower a flor
fly (insect) a mosca
fly v voar
food a comida
football [BE] o futebol
forecast a previsão
foreign o estrangeiro; ~ **currency** as divisas estrangeiras
forest a floresta
forget v esquecer
fork (utensil) o garfo; ~ **(in road)** a bifurcação
form o impresso
formula (baby) a papa
fortunately felizmente
fountain a fonte
free (available) livre; ~ **(no charge)** grátis
frequently muitas vezes, frequentemente
fresh fresco
friend o amigo, a amiga
full cheio
furniture a mobília

G

gallon o galão
game o jogo
garage a garagem
garbage bag o saco para o lixo
garden o jardim
gardener o jardineiro
gasoline a gasolina
gate (airport) a porta

gay club o clube gay
genuine autêntico, autêntica
get out v sair
gift a oferta
girl a menina
girlfriend a namorada
give v dar
give way (on the road) [BE] dar prioridade
glass (drinking) o copo
glass (material) o vidro
glove a luva
go ir
golf o golfe
good bom; ~ **morning** bom dia; ~**night** boa noite
goodbye adeus
gram o grama
grandparent o avô, a avó
grape a uva
gray o cinzento
green o verde
grocery store a mercearia
ground (camping) o terreno
group o grupo
guarantee a garantia
guide (person) o/a guia
guidebook o guia

H

hair o cabelo; ~ **gel** o gel para o cabelo; ~**brush** a escova de cabelo; ~**dryer** o secador de cabelo; ~**spray** a laca para o cabelo haircut o corte de cabelo

hairdresser (ladies/men) o cabeleireiro (senhoras/homens)

half metade

hammer o martelo

hand a mão

hand cream o creme para as mãos

hand luggage [BE] a bagagem de mão

handbag [BE] a mala de mão

handicapped o/a deficiente

handicapped accessible acessível a deficientes

hangover a ressaca

happy feliz

hat o chapéu

have v ter

head a cabeça

health a saúde

hear v ouvir

hearing aid o aparelho auditivo

heater o aquecedor

heating [BE] aquecedor

heavy pesado

height a altura

hello olá

help n a ajuda

help v ajudar

here aqui

high a altura

high tide a maré alta

highway a auto-estrada

hike (walk) o passeio a pé

hiking fazer longas caminhadas a pé

hill a colina

hire v [BE] alugar

hire car [BE] o carro de aluguer

hitchhike v pedir boleia

hold v (contain) conter

holiday o feriado

holiday [BE] as férias

home a casa

horse o cavalo

horseracing a corrida de cavalos

hospital o hospital

hostel a pensão

hot (temperature) quente; (spicy) picante

hot spring a nascente de água quente

hot water a água quente

hotel o hotel

hour a hora

house a casa

household goods os artigos para a casa

how (question) como

how much (question) quanto

hurt adj o ferido, a ferida

husband o marido

I

ice o gelo

ice cream o gelado, o sorvete; **~ parlor** a gelataria; **~ cone** o cone de gelado [sorvete]
ice hockey o hóquei no gelo
icy adj gelado, gelada
identification a identificação
ill adj o/a doente
illness a doença
in (place) no; **(time)** em
indoor dentro de casa; **~ pool** a piscina coberta
inexpensive barato
inflammation a inflamação
informal (dress) (o vestido) informal
information a informação
innocent o/a inocente
insect o insecto; **~ bite** a picada de insecto; **~ repellent** o repelente de insectos
inside dentro de
insomnia a insónia
instant coffee o café instantâneo
instant message a mensagem instantânea
insulin a insulina
insurance o seguro; **~ card** a apólice de seguro
interesting interessante
international internacional
internet cafe o internet café
internet service o serviço de internet

interpreter o/a intérprete
intersection o cruzamento
introduce v introduzir
invite v convidar
Ireland a Irlanda
Irish irlandês
iron v passar a ferro
island a ilha

J

jam doce
jar o frasco
jeans as calças de ganga
jellyfish a alforreca
jewelry as jóias
joke a piada
judge o juiz, a juiza
jumper cables os cabos da bateria

K

key a chave
key card o cartão da porta
kiddie pool a piscina de bebés
kilo(gram) o quilo(grama)
kilometer o quilómetro
kiosk o quiosque
kiss beijar
kitchen a cozinha
knee o joelho

L

lace a renda
ladder a escada
lake o lago

large grande
last o último
late (time) tarde; **(delayed)** atrasado
later mais tarde
launderette [BE] a lavandaria
laundromat a lavandaria
laundry service o serviço de lavandaria
lawyer o advogado, a advogada
learn v aprender
leather o cabedal
leave v partir
left a esquerda
left-luggage office [BE] o depósito de bagagem
lens a objectiva
less menos
lesson a lição
letter a carta
library a biblioteca
life a vida
lifeboat o barco salva-vidas
lifeguard o banheiro/salva-vidas
life jacket o colete salva-vidas
lift [BE] o elevador
light (shade) claro; **(weight)** leve
light n a luz; v ascender
lightbulb a lâmpada (eléctrica)
lighter o isqueiro
lightning o relâmpago
line (waiting) a fila (de espera)
line (subway) a linha

linen o linho
lip o lábio
liquor store a loja de bebidas alcoólicas
liter o litro
little pequeno, pequena
live v viver
local regional
lock n a fechadura
locked adj fechado, fechada
locker o cacifo com fecho
log on v autenticar
log off v sair
long comprido; **(time)** muito
long-sighted [BE] visto de longe
look v ver
look for procurar
lose v perder
lost adj perdido
lost-and-found os perdidos e achados
lotion a loção
louder mais alto
love (a person) amar; **(a thing)** gostar de
luggage a bagagem
luggage cart [trolley] o carrinho
luggage locker o cacifo de bagagem
luggage ticket o talão de bagagem
lumpy (mattress) aos altos e baixos

lunch o almoço
lung o pulmão

M

magazine a revista
magnificent magnífico, magnífica
mail o correio
mailbox a caixa do correio
main course o prato principal
make up a prescription [BE] receitar
male o homem
man o homem
manager o/a gerente
manicure a manicure
manual (gears) (a caixa de velocidades) manual map o mapa
market o mercado
married casado
mass (church service) a missa
massage a massagem
matches (fire) os fósforos
material o material
mattress o colchão
maybe talvez
meal a refeição
mean v significar
measure v medir
measurement o tamanho
meat a carne
medicine o remédio
medium (size) médio; **(cooked)** meio-passado

meet v encontrar(-se)
mend v consertar
menu o menu
message a mensagem
metal o metal
meter (taxi) o taxímetro
meter (parking) o parquímetro
microwave (oven) o microondas
midday [BE] o meio-dia
migraine a enxaqueca
mileage a quilometragem
minibar o mini-bar
minute o minuto
mirror o espelho
miss v perder
missing em falta
mistake o engano
misunderstanding o mal-entendido
mobile phone [BE] o telemóvel
mobile home a casa ambulante
modern moderno, moderna
money o dinheiro
monument o monumento
moped a lambreta
more mais
mosquito o mosquito
mother a mãe
motion sickness o enjoo
motor o motor
motorbike a motocicleta
motorboat o barco a motor
motorway [BE] a auto-estrada
mountain a montanha; ~

bike a bicicleta de montanha
moustache o bigode
mouth a boca
move v mudar(-se)
movie o filme
movie theater o cinema
much muito
mug (drinking) a caneca
mugging o assalto
mumps a papeira
museum o museu
music a música

N

nail (body) a unha; ~polish o
   verniz de unhas
name o nome
napkin o guardanapo
nappy [BE] a fralda
narrow estreito
national nacional
nationality a nacionalidade
nature preserve a reserva
   natural
nausea a náusea
near perto
nearest mais próximo
necessary necessário
neck (body) o pescoço;
   (clothing) a gola
necklace o colar
needle a agulha
neighbor o vizinho, a vizinha
nephew o sobrinho
never nunca

new novo, nova
newspaper o jornal
newsstand [newsagent] o
   quiosque de jornais
next próximo, próxima
next to ao lado de
niece a sobrinha
night a noite
nightclub o nightclub
no não
no one ninguém
noisy barulhento
non-alcoholic não-
   alcoólico, não-alcoólica
non-smoking adj não-
   fumadores
none nenhum, nenhuma
normal normal
north o norte
note a nota
note [BE] a nota
notebook o caderno
nothing nada
now agora
number (telephone) o número
   de telefone
number plate (car) [BE] a
   placa de matrícula
nurse o enfermeiro, a
   enfermeira

O

observatory o observatório
occupied ocupado, ocupada
off-licence [BE] a loja de vinhos

office o escritório
often muitas vezes
oil o óleo
okay O.K.
old o velho, a velha
old-fashioned antigo, antiga
one um, uma
one-way ticket o bilhete de ida
open v abrir
open adj aberto, aberta
opening hours as horas de funcionamento
opera a ópera
operation a operação
opposite o oposto
optician o oculista
orange (fruit) a laranja; **(color)** cor-de-laranja
orchestra a orquestra
order v encomendar
outdoor ao ar livre; ~ **pool** a piscina ao ar livre
outside fora de
over sobre
overdone adj cozido demais
overnight só uma noite

P

pacifier a chupeta
pack v fazer as malas
package o embrulho
paddling pool [BE] a piscina de bebés
padlock o cadeado
pain a dor

paint v pintar
painter o pintor, a pintora
painting o quadro
pajamas o pijama
palace o palácio
pants as calças
pantyhose os collants
paper o papel
paper napkin o guardanapo de papel
park o parque
park v estacionar
parking o estacionamento; ~ **lot** o parque de estacionamento; ~ **meter** o parquímetro; ~ **space** o lugar de estacionamento
partner o companheiro, a companheira
part a peça
party a festa
pass n o passe
pass v passar
passenger o passageiro, a passageira
passport o passaporte
pastry shop a pastelaria
patch v remendar
path o caminho
pay v pagar
pay phone o telefone público
peak (mountain) o pico
pearl a pérola
pedestrian crossing a passadeira

pedicure a pedicure
pen a caneta
pencil o lápis
penicillin a penicilina
per por: ~ **day** por dia; ~
  hour por hora; ~ **night** por
  noite; ~ **week** por semana
performance a sessão
perfume o perfume
perhaps talvez
period período
permit a permissão; v permitir
petrol [BE] a gasolina; ~
  station [BE] a bomba de
  gasolina
pharmacy a farmácia
phone o telefone; ~ **call** o
  telefonema; ~ **card** o
  credifone
photo a fotografia
photocopier a fotocopiadora
photographer o fotógrafo, a
  fotógrafa
photography a fotografia
pick up v ir buscar;
  (collect) levantar
picnic o piquenique; ~ **area** a
  área para piqueniques
piece a peça
pill (birth control) a pílula
pillow a almofada
personal identification
  number (PIN) o PIN
pink cor-de-rosa
piste [BE] a pista; ~ **map**

  [BE] o mapa de pistas
pizzeria a pizzaria
place o lugar; **(a bet)** apostar
plane o avião
plant a planta
plastic wrap o papel aderente
plate o prato
platform [BE] a linha
platinum a platina
play v jogar; **(instrument)** tocar
please se faz favor
plug (electric) a ficha (eléctrica)
plunger o desentupidor
pocket o bolso
poison o veneno
police a polícia; ~ **report** o
  documento da polícia; ~
  station a esquadra da polícia
pond a lagoa
pool a piscina
pop music a música pop
popcorn as pipocas
popular popular
port (harbor) o porto
Portugal Portugal
Portuguese português
post [BE] o correio; ~ **office** os
  correios
postbox [BE] a caixa do correio
postcard o postal
poster o cartaz
pottery a cerâmica
pound (British sterling) a libra
  (esterlina)
pregnant a grávida

prescribe prescrever
prescription a receita
press v (clothing) passar a ferro
pretty bonito, bonita
print v imprimir
problem o problema
prohibit proibido
pronounce v pronunciar
public o público
pull v puxar
pump a bomba; (gas) a bomba de gasolina
puncture [BE] o furo

Q

quality a qualidade
question a pergunta
queue [BE] n a fila
quiet sossegado, sossegada

R

race (cars, horses) a corrida; ~ track o hipódromo
racket (sports) a raquete
railway station [BE] a estação de caminhos de ferro
rain v chover
raincoat a gabardine
rape a violação
rare (unusual) raro, rara; (steak) mal-passado, mal-passada
razor a navalha; ~ blade a lâmina de barbear

read v ler
ready pronto, pronta
real (genuine) de lei
receipt a factura
reception (desk) a recepção
receptionist o/a recepcionista
recommend v recomendar
red vermelho, vermelha
refrigerator o frigorífico
region a região
regular (gas/petrol) normal
rent v alugar
rental car o carro alugado
repair v arranjar
repeat v repetir
reservation a marcação
reserve v reservar
restaurant o restaurante
restroom a casa de banho
return v (come back) voltar; (give back) devolver
right (correct) certo; ~ of way prioridade
ring o anel
river o rio
road a estrada
robbed roubado, roubada
robbery o roubo
romantic romântico
room o quarto; ~ service o serviço de quarto
round redondo, redonda
round-trip de ida e volta
route o caminho

owboat o barco a remos

ubbish [BE] o lixo; ~ **bin** [BE] o caixote do lixo

uins as ruínas

ad triste

afe n o cofre; adj seguro

afety a segurança

ales tax IVA

ame o mesmo, a mesma

and a areia

andals as sandálias

anitary napkin o penso higiénico

aucepan o tacho

auna o sauna

ave guardar

avings account a conta de poupança

canner o scanner

carf o lenço de pescoço

chedule o horário

chool a escola

cissors a tesoura

ea o mar

eat o lugar

ee ver

elf-service self-service

ell v vender

end v mandar

enior citizen o reformado, a reformada

eparated separado, separada

erious sério, séria

service charge a taxa de serviço

set menu a ementa turística

sex o sexo

sexually transmitted disease (STD) Doença Sexualmente Transmissível (DST)

shallow pouco fundo, funda

shampoo o shampoo

sharp afiado, afiada

shaving cream o creme da barba

sheet o lençol

ship o navio

shirt a camisa

shoe o sapato; ~ **store** a sapataria

shopping compras; ~ **area** a zona comercial; ~ **centre** [BE] o centro comercial; ~ **mall** o centro comercial

short curto

shorts os calções

short sighted [BE] de vistas curtas

show n o espectáculo; v mostrar

shower o chuveiro

sick doente

side (of road) o lado; ~**effect** o efeito secundário; ~ **order** à parte; ~ **street** transversal

sidewalk o passeio

sightseeing tour o circuito turístico

sign o sinal

silk a seda

silver a prata

single (not married) solteiro; ~ **room** o quarto individual

sink o lava-louças

sister a irmã

sit v sentar(-se)

size o número/tamanho

skin a pele

skirt a saia

skis os skis

sleep dormir

sleeping bag o saco-cama

sleeper car [BE] couchette

slice a fatia

slippers os chinelos

slope (ski) a rampa

slow lento, lenta

slower mais devagar

slowly devagar

small pequeno, pequena

small change troco

smoke v fumar

smoking (area) zona de fumadores

snack bar o snack bar, a cafetaria

sneakers as sapatilhas [os ténis]

snorkel mergulho sem garrafa [snorkel]

snow a neve; v nevar

snowboard a prancha de snowboard

soap o sabonete

soccer o futebol

sock a peúga, meia

soft drink (soda) o refresco

sold out a lotação esgotada

someone alguém

something alguma coisa

sometimes às vezes

son o filho

sore throat a dor de garganta

sorry desculpe

south sul

souvenir a lembrança

spa o spa

speak falar

speed limit o limite de velocidade

speed v ir com excesso de velocidade

spell soletrar

spend gastar

spine a espinha

sponge a esponja

sport o desporto

sporting goods store a loja de artigos de desporto

spring a primavera

square o quadrado

stadium o estádio

stairs as escadas

stamp o selo

start começar

starter [BE] hors-d'oeuvre, o aperitivo

station a estação

station wagon a carrinha
statue a estátua
stay permanecer
steal roubar
steep íngreme
sting o espeto
stolen roubado
stomach o estômago
stop n (bus, tram) a paragem
stop v parar
store guide a planta da loja
storey [BE] o prédio
straight ahead sempre em frente
stream o ribeiro
street a estrada
stroller a cadeira de bebé
student o/a estudante
study v estudar
subway o metro; ~ station a estação de metro
suit o fato
suitcase a mala de viagem
sun o sol
sun block o protector solar
sunbathe tomar banho de sol
sunburn a queimadura de sol
sunglasses os óculos de sol
super (fuel) super
supermarket o supermercado
surfboard a prancha de surf
sweatshirt a sweatshirt
sweet (taste) doce
sweets [BE] os rebuçados
swim v nadar

swimsuit o fato de banho
symbol o símbolo
synagogue a sinagoga

T

table a mesa
tablet (medicine) o comprimido
take v (carry) levar; (medicine) tomar; (time) demorar
take away [BE] para levar
tampons os tampões higiénicos
taste v provar
taxi o táxi; ~ stand a praça de táxis
team a equipa
teaspoon a colher de chá
telephone o telefone
tennis o ténis
tent a tenda; ~ peg a cavilha; ~ pole a estaca
terminal (airport) o terminal
text v (send a message) escrever uma mensagem; n (message) texto
thank you obrigado
that esse, essa
theater teatro
theft roubo
there ali
thief ladrão
thigh coxa
thirsty com sede

this este, esta
throat a garganta
ticket o bilhete; ~ **machine** a máquina de venda de bilhetes; ~ **office** a bilheteira [a bilheteria]
tie (clothing) a gravata
time as horas
timetable [BE] o horário
tire o pneu
tired cansado, cansada
tissue o lenço de papel
today hoje
toe o dedo do pé
together juntos
toilet a casa de banho
toilet paper o papel higiénico
tomorrow amanhã
tongue a língua
tonight hoje à noite; **for ~** para hoje à noite
too (much) demasiado; **(also)** também
tooth o dente
toothbrush a escova de dentes
toothpaste a pasta de dentes
tour avisita
tourist o/a turista
towel a toalha
town a cidade; ~ **hall** a câmara municipal; ~ **map** o mapa de cidade
toy o brinquedo
toy store o armazém de brinquedos

track o trilho
traffic o trânsito; ~ **jam** o engarrafamento; ~ **circle** a rotunda; ~ **light** o semáforo
trail o caminho; ~ **map** o mapa
train o comboio; ~ **station** a estação de caminho de ferro
transfer (plane, train) o transbordo
translate v traduzir
trash o lixo; ~ **can** a lixeira
travel v viajar; ~ **agency** a agência de viagens
traveler's check o cheque de viagens
tree a árvore
trip a excursão
trolley o carrinho
trousers [BE] as calças
T-shirt a T-Shirt
TV a televisão
type o tipo
tyre [BE] o pneu

U

ugly feio, feia
umbrella (rain) o guarda-chuva
unbranded medication [BE] o medicamento genérico
uncle o tio
unconscious perder os sentidos
underground [BE] o metropolitano; ~ **station [BE]** a estação de

motropolitano

underpants as cuecas
understand compreende
United Kingdom o Reino Unido
United States os Estados
  Unidos
university a universidade
unleaded (gas) sem chumbo
unlimited (mileage) sem
  limite (de quilometragem)
unlock v abrir
upper superior
upstairs em cima
use v usar
use n uso
useful útil
username o nome de utilizador
utensil o utensílio

V

vacancy o quarto vago
vacation as férias
vaccination a vacinação
vacuum cleaner o aspirador
vagina a vagina
valid válido
valley o vale
valuable de valor
value o valor
VAT (sales tax) IVA
vegetarian vegetariano
vehicle o veículo; ~
  registration os documentos
  do carro
veterinarian o veterinário a

veterinária

view point [BE] o miradouro
village a aldeia
vineyard a vinha
visa o visto
visit n a visita
visit v visitar
visitor center o centro de
  acolhimento
visually impaired os invisuais
vitamin a vitamina
volleyball o voleibol
vomit vomitar

W

wait esperar
waiting room a sala de espera
waiter o empregado
waitress a empregada
wake-up call a chamada para
  despertar
walk v dar um passeio
walking passear
walking route o itinerário a pé
wall a parede
wallet a carteira (de
  documentos)
warm adj morno, morna;
  v aquecer
wash v lavar
washing machine a máquina
  de lavar
watch n o relógio; v ver
water a água
water skis os skis aquáticos

weather o tempo; ~ **forecast** a previsão do tempo

wedding o casamento; ~ **ring** a aliança

week a semana

weekend o fim-de-semana

weekly (ticket) semanal

welcome benvindo, benvinda

west oeste

what que

wheelchair a cadeira de rodas; ~ **ramp** a rampa para cadeira de rodas

when quando

where onde

white branco, branca

who quem

wife a mulher

window a janela; **(store)** a montra

window seat o lugar à janela

windshield o pára-brisas

windsurfer a prancha à vela

wireless sem fios; ~ **internet** internet sem fios; ~ **internet service** serviço de internet sem fios; ~ **phone** telephone sem fios

with com

without sem

woman a mulher

wool a lã

work v **(job)** trabalhar; **(function)** funcionar

wrap v embrulhar

wrist o pulso

write v escrever

wrong errado, errada

Y

year o ano

yellow amarelo, amarela

yes sim

young jovem

youth hostel a pousada da juventude

Z

zebra crossing [BE] a passadeira

zero zero

zone a zona

zoo o jardim zoológico, o zoo

PORTUGUESE–ENGLISH

A

à tarde p.m.
a abadia abbey
o abajur lampshade
aberto open
o abraço hug
abril April
acampar camp
o acesso para deficientes access for handicapped
achados e perdidos lost and found
o acrílico acrylic
o açúcar sugar
adiante ahead
a admissão admissions
o advogado attorney
o aeroporto airport
a agência de câmbio currency exchange office
a agência de viagens travel agent
agora now
agosto August
a água potável drinking water
o albergue de juventude youth hostel
a aldeia village
a alergia allergy
alérgico allergic
a alfândega customs

o algodão cotton
alguém someone
o alojamento accommodations
alpinismo mountaineering
aluga-se for rent
alugam-se carros car rental
aluguer de bicicletas bicycle rental
amanhã tomorrow
a ambulância ambulance
o andebol handball
antiguidades antiques
aquecer warm
a areia sand
o armazém department store
o ascensor elevator
o aspirador vacuum
a assinatura signature
atender answer
o atendimento admissions
o atendimento ao cliente customer service
atrasado delayed
o atrelado trailer
a auto-estrada highway [motorway]
o autocarro bus
automático automatic
o automóvel car
o avião plane
o aviso warning

B

a bagagem baggage [luggage]
o balcão de registo check-in counter
o balcão de informações information desk
o banco bank
o banho bath
o barbeiro barber
o barco boat
o barco salva-vidas lifeboat
o basebol baseball
o basquetebol basketball
o beijo kiss
bemvindo welcome
a biblioteca library
a bicicleta bicycle
o bilhete electrónico e-ticket
o bilhete semanal weekly ticket
a bilheteira ticket office
o bilhete ticket
os bolsos pockets
a bomba pump
a bomba de gasolina gas [petrol] station
os bombeiros fire department [brigade]
as botas de ski ski boots
o boxe boxing
o briberom baby bottle

C

o cabeleireiro hairdresser
o cabeleireiro de homens barber
o cabelo hair
a cadeira de rodas wheelchair
a caixa cashier
o calçado shoes
acalculadora calculator
o calor heat
as calorias calories
a câmara municipal town hall
o câmbio currency exchange office
o camião truck
o caminho path
a camioneta bus [coach]
o camping campsite
o campo de desportos playing field
a cana de pesca fishing rod
o canal canal
cancelado canceled
o candeeiro lamp
o capacete helmet
a capela chapel
o carnaval carnival
a carne meat
o carro car
a carta regist[r]ada registered letter
o cartão business card
a carteira wallet
a casa house
a casa de banho bathroom
a casa de câmbio currency exchange office

o **casaco** coat
o **castelo** castle
a **catedral** cathedral
o **cavalo** horse
a **caverna** cave
o **cemitério** cemetery
o **cêntimo** cent
o **centro comercial** shopping mall [shopping centre]
o **centro da cidade** downtown area
o **centro desportivo** sports center
o **centro do povo** town square
a **cerveja** beer
o **chá** tea
o **chalé** cottage
a **chamada gratuita** toll-free call
a **charcutaria** delicatessen
a **chave** key
as **chegadas** arrivals (airport)
a **chupeta** pacifier
o **churrasco** barbecue
a **chuva** rain
o **chuveiro** shower
a **cidade** city
a **cidade antiga** old town
o **cigarro** cigarette
o **cinema** movie theater [cinema]
a **cirurgia** surgery
a **clínica de saúde** health clinic
o **cobre** copper
o **código de área** area code

o **colete de salvação** life jacket
a **colina** hill
com with
com chumbo leaded
o **comboio rápido** express train
o **comboio suburbano** local train
o **combustível** fuel
completo full
o **comprimido** pill
o **computador** computer
a **comunhão** communion
o **condicionador** conditioner
a **confeitaria** pastry shop
congelado frozen
os **consertos** repairs
constipado constipated
a **conta corrente** checking [current] account
a **conta de poupança** savings account
o **conteúdo** contents
o **controle de passaportes** passport control
o(s) **correio(s)** post office
o **correio azul** express mail
o **correio normal** regular mail
a **corrente** lock
os **cosméticos** cosmetics
a **costa** coast
o **couro** leather
o **credifone** phone card
a **criança** child
o **cuidado** caution

os cuidados intensivos intensive care

D

a dança dance
a data date
a data de nascimento date of birth
de ida e volta round-trip [return]
o dentista dentist
a depilação a cera waxing
o depósito refund
o depósito de bagagem baggage check
descartável disposable
o desconto discount
o desembarque arrivals (airport)
o desentupidor plunger
o deserto desert
despachar check (baggage)
o desporto sports
o destino destination
o desvio detour [diversion]
o detergente detergent
devagar slow
a devolução refund
Dezembro December
os dias úteis weekdays
os dicionários dictionaries
a dieta diet
o dietético health food
digital digital
o dique dam
a direcção address

dirija com cuidado drive carefully
dissolver dissolve
a distância distance
os doces candy [sweets]
os documentos de registo registration papers
doméstico domestic
o domingo Sunday
a dor pain
a drogaria drugstore
a duna dune

E

o elevador elevator
em construção under construction
em serviço occupied
a embaixada embassy
a embalagem perdida non-returnable
o embarque departures (airport)
a ementa menu
a ementa turística tourist menu
a emergência emergency
empurrar push
encerrado closed
a encosta perigosa dangerous slope
o endereço address
engraçado cute
a enseada bay
a entrada entrance

a entrada proibida no entry
entrar enter
a entrega de bagagem baggage claim
as entregas deliveries
o equipamento de mergulho diving equipment
os equipamentos eletrónicos electronic goods
o ervanário health food store
a escada rolante escalator
as escadas stairs
escalar climbing
a escarpa cliff
a escola school
o escritório de achados e perdidos lost-and-found office
a especialidade da casa house specialty
a especialidade da região local specialty
o espectáculo show
o espectador spectator
a esquadra da polícia police station
esta noite this evening
a estação station
a estação de caminhos de ferro train station
a estação de metro subway station
a estação de serviço gas [petrol] station

a estação rodoviária bus [coach] station
o estacionamento parking lot [car park]
o estacionamento para clientes customer parking
estacione aqui park here
o estádio stadium
a estância turística tourist resort
o estanho can
a estátua statue
a estrada road
a estrada em construção road under construction
a estrada fechada road closed
o estrangeiro foreign
a estreia premiere
o estreitamento de rua narrow road
o estuário estuary
exclusivo para residentes residents only
exclusivo para pedestres pedestrians only
exclusivo para pessoal autorizado authorized vehicles only
a excursão tour
exige-se a identificação proof of identity required
a exposição exhibition
o extintor (de incêndios) fire extinguisher

F

a **fábrica** factory
a **fábrica manual** made by hand
fala-se inglês English spoken
a **farmácia** drugstore
o **farol** lighthouse
a **febre** fever
fechado closed
a **feira** fair
a **feira popular** amusement park
feito à mão handmade
o **feriado nacional** national holiday
Fevereiro February
o **fim** end
o **fim de auto-estrada** end of highway [motorway]
a **floresta** forest
o/a **florista** florist
o **fogo de artifício** fireworks
a **fonte** fountain
a **forma** form
a **fortaleza** fortress
o **forte** fort
a **fotocópia** photocopy
a **fotografia** photography
a **fralda** diaper [nappy]
a **frente** front
fresco fresh
a **fronteira** border crossing
a **fruta** fruit
fumar *v* smoke

os **fumadores** smoking (area)
o **futebol** soccer [football]
o **futebol americano** American football

G

a **galeria de arte** art gallery
a **garagem** garage
a **garantia** guarantee
a **gare** platforms
a **gasolina** gas [petrol]
genuino genuine
o/a **gerente** manager
o **ginásio** gym
o **glúten** gluten
o **golfe** golf
a **gota** drop
grande large
grátis free
gratuito free
a **gravata** tie
a **grávida** pregnant
a **grelha de churrasco** barbecue
o **grelhado** grilled
a **gruta** cave
guardar save
o **guia de viagem** travel guide

H

o **helicóptero** helicopter
o **hipismo** horseback riding
o **hipódromo** racetrack [racecourse]
hoje today

o hóquei hockey

o hóquei no gelo ice hockey

o horário schedule [timetable]

o horário comercial business hours

o horário de abertura opening hours

o horário de visitas visiting hours

o hospital hospital

o hotel hotel

I

ida e volta round-trip [return]

a igreja church

a ilha island

o IVA imposto de venda sales tax [VAT]

incluído included

incluído no preço included in the price

o indicativo code

o infantário kindergarten

as informações information

as informações turísticas tourist information

o ingrediente ingredient

o início de auto-estrada highway [motorway] entrance

inocente innocent

inquebrável unbreakable

inserir v insert

insosso bland

as instruções instructions

integral whole wheat

interdito ao trânsito traffic-free zone

interessado interested

internacional international

introduzir introduce

o inverno winter

o IVA sales tax [VAT]

J

Janeiro January

a janela window

o jardim garden

o jardim botânico botanical garden

o jardim zoológico zoo

a joalharia jeweler

o jogo match

Julho July

Junho June

L

a lã wool

o lago lake

a lancha motorboat

os lanches snacks

o largo square

os lacticínios dairy products

a lavagem de carros car wash

a lavagem de roupa laundry facilities

a lavandaria laundromat [launderette]

la avandaria a seco dry-cleaner

lavar a seco dry-clean only
lavável à máquina machine washable
a lembrança souvenir
a lente lens
as lições lessons
a lima nail file
o limite da cidade city limits
o limite de bagagem baggage allowance
a limpeza cleaning
a língua language
a língua estrangeira foreign language
a linha platform
a linha aérea airline
a linha de bonde tram
a linha férrea railroad [railway]
a liquidação clearance sale
o líquido liquid
Lisboa Lisbon
a lista menu
a lista telefónica directory
a lista de preços price list
o litoral coast
a livraria bookstore
livre vacant
o livrete car registration papers
o loção para depois da barba after-shave lotion
a loja de antiguidades antique store
a loja de artigos de desporto sporting goods store
a loja de brinquedos toy store

a loja de departamentos department store
as lojas duty-free duty-free store
a lotação esgotada sold out
a lotaria lottery
a louça china
o lugar à janela window seat
o lugar na asa aisle seat
o luxo luxury

M

a madeira wood
as madeixas highlights
o maestro conductor
magro fat-free
Maio May
mais more
mais devagar slower
mais rápido faster
as malas luggage [baggage]
mandar send
os mandriões loafers
o mapa da cidade city map
o mapa dos arredores area map
a máquina fotográfica camera
o mar sea
Março March
as massas noodles
a mata wood
a maternidade maternity
a matrícula do automóvel license plate [registration] number

o **médico** doctor
médio medium
o **menu** menu
o **menu turístico** tourist menu
o **mercado** market
as **mercadorias** goods
as **mercadorias isentas** duty-free goods
a **mercearia** grocer
mergulhar diving
o **metro** subway [underground]
a **mina** mine
a **missa** mass
o **mobiliário** furniture
a **moeda** coin
o **moinho** mill
o **moinho de vento** windmill
molhada wet
o **molusco** shellfish
a **montanha** mountain
o **montanhismo** mountaineering
o **monte** hill
o **monumento** monument
o **monumento comemorativo (war)** memorial
o **mosteiro** monastery
a **moto de montanha** mountain bike
a **motorizada** motorcycle
os **móveis** furniture
as **mudanças** manual shift
a **mudança de óleo** oil change
mudar change
a **mulher** woman

a **muralha da cidade** city wall
o **muro** wall
o **museu** museum
a **música** music
a **música ao vivo** live music
a **música clássica** classical music
a **música folk** folk music
a **música pop** pop music

N

nacional national
nacionalidade nationality
nada a declarar nothing to declare
não entre keep out
não fumadores non-smokers
não fumar no smoking
não funciona out of order
o **Natal** Christmas
navegação à vela sailing
o **navio** ship
a **neve** snow
o **nome** name
a **nome de família** last name
o **nome de solteira** maiden name
Novembro November
novo new
as **nozes** nuts
o **número de telefone** telephone number
o **número do passaporte** passport number

O

as obras construction
o oculista optician
ocupado occupied
a oferta especial special offer
a oficina office
o óleo oil
o operador operator
a ordem de pagamento money order
a orquestra orchestra
a ourivesaria goldsmith
o ouro gold
o outono fall [autumn]
Outubro October

P

o paço palace
a padaria bakery
o país country
o palácio palace
o palácio da justiça law court
o palco stage
o pão bread
o papel higiénico toilet paper
o papel reciclado recycled paper
a papelaria stationery store
para microondas microwaveable
para uso externo external use only
a paragem de autocarro bus stop

o parapente gliding
o pára-quedas parachuting
pare stop
a parede wall
o parque park
o parque de campismo campsite
o parque de diversões amusement park
o parque de estacionamento parking lot [car park]
o parque nacional national park
o parque para clientes customer parking
o parque privativo private parking
as partidas departures (airport)
as partidas internacionais international departures
a Páscoa Easter
a passadeira crosswalk [zebra crossing]
o passageiro passenger
as passagens (airplane) tickets
o passaporte passport
o passe mensal monthly ticket
o passeio walkway
o passeio panorâmico scenic route
o passeio a cavalo horseback riding
o passeio com guia guided tour
o passeio circular round trip

a **pastelaria** pastry shop
a **pastilha** lozenge
a **patinagem no gelo** ice skating
os **patins** skates
o **pediatra** pediatrician
a **pedicure** pedicure
o **peito** chest
a **peixaria** fish store [fishmonger]
a **pensão** bed & breakfast
os **peões** pedestrian
pequeno small
o **pequeno-almoço** breakfast
o **percurso da natureza** nature trail
o **percurso de bicicleta** bike trail
o **percurso panorâmico** scenic route
perdido lost
o **perigo** danger
perigoso dangerous
permanecer v stay
a **pérola** pearl
perto near
a **pesca** fishing
o **pico** peak
a **pílula** pill
o **PIN** PIN
pintado de fresco wet paint
a **piscina** swimming pool
o **planador** gliding
o **planetário** planetarium
o **pneu** tire [tyre]

o **poço** well
pode cozinhar cooking facilities
a **polícia** police
a **polícia de trânsito** traffic police
a **poltrona** seat
a **pomada** ointment
o **pomar** orchard
a **ponte** bridge
a **ponte baixa** low bridge
a **ponte estreita** narrow bridge
a **ponte levadiça** drawbridge
por favor please
a **porta** door
o **porta-moedas** purse
a **porta de embarque** boarding gate
a **porta de incêndio** fire door
a **portagem** toll
o **portão** gate
a **porta automática** automatic door
o **porto** port
o **posto de ambulância** ambulance station
a **pousada** guest house
o **povoado** village
a **praça** square
a **praça de táxis** taxi stand
a **praia** beach
a **praia de nudismo** nudist beach
a **prancha de surf[e]** surfboard

a prata silver
o prato do dia dish of the day
o preço price
preferencial yield [give way]
a primavera spring
a primeira classe first class
o primeiro nome first name
os primeiros socorros first aid
a prioridade priority
privado private
os produtos de limpeza cleaning products
o produto dietético health food
proibida a entrada no entry
proibido forbidden
proibido acampar no camping
proibido estacionar no parking
proibido fumar no smoking
o pronto socorro-emergência accident and emergency
o propósito purpose
provar v taste
o próximo next
puxar pull

Q

a quantia fare
quarta-feira Wednesday
o quartel de bombeiros fire station
o quarto duplo double room
o quarto para alugar room to rent
quatro estrelas four star
a queda de água waterfall

a queda de pedras falling rocks
o quilómetro kilometer
a quinta farm
quinta-feira Thursday
o quiosque de jornais newsagent

R

os raios-x x-ray
a rampa ramp
a receita federal customs control
a recepção reception
o recibo receipt
reciclado recycled
reduza a velocidade slow down
o reembolso refund
as refeições meals
o regente conductor (music)
a região region
o relicário shrine
as reparações repairs (car)
a represa dam
o rés-do-chão first floor
reservado reserved
a reserva reservation
o reservatório reservoir
residencial guest house
o restaurante restaurant
retire fundos withdraw money
retire o bilhete take ticket
retornar v return
a revista magazine
a ribeira stream

o rio river

o rochedo cliff

o rolo film (camera)

a rota alternada alternate route

a rotunda traffic circle [roundabout]

a roupa interior underwear

a rua street

a rua fechada ao trânsito road closed

a rua principal main road

a rua com sentido único one-way street

as ruinas ruins

S

sábado Saturday

o sabonete soap

o saco bag

a saída exit

a saída de emergência emergency exit

o sal salt

a sala de operações operating room

s sala de concertos concert hall

s sala de espera waiting room

o saldo sale

a salsicharia delicatessen

o salva-vidas lifeguards

o sapato shoe

a sé cathedral

o secador de cabelo hair dryer

a seda silk

a segunda classe second class

o segundo andar second floor

segunda-feira Monday

os segundos seconds

a segurança security

o seguro insurance

o selo stamp

sem açúcar sugar-free

sem álcool alcohol-free

sem cafeína caffeine-free

sem chumbo unleaded

sem gordura fat-free

sem sal salt-free

o semáforo traffic light

a semana week

a senha ticket

as senhoras ladies

a serra mountain range

o serviço service charge

o serviço a clientes customer service

o serviço de quarto room service

o serviço incluído service included

Setembro September

sexta-feira Friday

o silêncio silence

só com dinheiro cash only

a sobremesa dessert

a soirée evening performance

o solário sun lounge

o solo escorregadio slippery road surface

o **solteiro** single (room)
a **sopa** soup
sos emergency services
o **spa** spa
o **supermercado** supermarket

T

os **talheres** utensils [cutlery]
o **talho** butcher
a **tarifa** rate
a **tarifa mínima** minimum charge
a **taxa de serviço** service charge
o **táxi** taxi
o **taxímetro** taxi meter
o **teatro** theater
o **teatro ao ar livrea** open-air theater
o **teatro infantil** children´s theater
o **teleférico** chair lift
o **telefone** telephone
o **telefone de emergência** emergency telephone
o **telefone público** public telephone
o **telefone residencial** home phone number
os **temperos** spices
a **tenda** tent
o **ténis** tennis
a **terapia intensiva** intensive care
terça-feira Tuesday

o **terminal** terminal
a **tipografia** printing
as **toalhas** linen
tóxico toxic
o **tráfego lento** slow traffic
o **trajecto do autocarro** bus route
o **trampolim** diving board
transferir transfer
o **trânsito impedido** closed to traffic
transportar carry
o **tratamento** treatment
o **travão** brake
o **travão de emergência** emergency brake
o **trigo** wheat
o **trolley-carro** tram
o **túnel** tunnel
o **turismo** tourist information office

U

a **universidade** university
os **utensílios de cozinha** kitchen equipment
os **utensílios domésticos** household goods

V

o **vagão-cama** sleeping car
o **vagão restaurante** dining car
vago vacant
o **vale** valley
o **vale postal** money order

válido valid
a varanda balcony
os vegetais vegetables
o veículo vehicle
o veículo lento slow vehicle
o veleiro sailboat
a velocidade máxima maximum speed limit
a venda de bilhetes ticket office
venenoso poisonous
o verão summer
o verdadeiro real
o vestuário fitting room
a via de dois sentidos two-way traffic
a via de sentido único one-way street
a via rápida highway [motorway]
a via turística scenic route

o vidro glass
o vidro reciclado recycled glass
a vila town
o vilarejo village
as vinhas vineyard
o vinho do porto port (wine)
o vinho wine
a visita guiada guided tour
o voleibol volleyball
o vôo flight

Z

a zona aduaneira customs zone
a zona comercial business district
a zona de pedestres pedestrian zone
a zona histórica historic area
a zona residencial residential zone